The Wine Lover's Dessert Cookbook

Savor Lifes Sweet Pleasures!

Mary Cech

The Wine Lover's Dessert Cookbook

recipes and pairings for the perfect glass of wine

• • •

BY MARY CECH AND JENNIE SCHACHT

"A WORLD TOUR OF DESSERT WINES" BY TIM PATTERSON

PHOTOGRAPHS BY FRANKIE FRANKENY

CHRONICLE BOOKS

SAN FRANCISCO

Library of Congress Cataloging-in-Publication Data available. ISBN 0-8118-4237-1

Manufactured in China.

Prop styling by Diane Gsell and JoAnn Frankeny

Food styling by Diane Gsell

Designed by Em Dash

Distributed in Canada by Raincoast Books, 9050 Shaughnessy Street, Vancouver, British Columbia V6P 6E5

10 9 8 7 6 5 4 3 2 1

Chronicle Books LLC, 85 Second Street, San Francisco, California 94105

www.chroniclebooks.com

page 7: Caramel Macadamia Tart, page 149

To the greatest culinary influence in my life, Albert Kumin.

—*Mary*

To my parents, who taught me to do good, and to Birdi, who taught me the goodness of indulgence. She would never hesitate to eat dessert first.

—*Jennie*

Acknowledgments

This book would not have been possible without the assistance and enthusiasm of so many friends and colleagues. We thank first and foremost our outstanding team of recipe testers, who diligently prepared the desserts and offered feedback that ensures the recipes are delivered to you in top-notch condition. They include Maria August, Pilar Beccar-Varela, Bob Birge, Ruth Brousseau, Sue Burish, John Connell, Martha Curti, Angela Davies, Marjorie Goldfarb, Delia Gummere, Linda Hillel, Morgen Humes, Dan and Laura Leff, Emily Lichtenstein, Nancy Nottage, Elizabeth Perreault, Karl Rimbach, and Sandy Sonnenfelt. A special thanks to those testers who went to extra lengths—testing numerous recipes, hosting wine and dessert tastings, offering advice in great detail, and in so many other ways: Jane Boaz, Mary Davis, Marilyn and Lynn Davison, Jessica Reich, and Linda Yoshino. Nancy Kux, Marie Simmons, and Micki Weinberg were a great help in divulging the secrets of chocolate, eggs, and other ingredients.

For their editorial suggestions, we thank John Birdsall, Linda Carucci, Jill Hough, Randy Milden, Elizabeth Thomas, and Laura Werlin. Special thanks to our copyeditor, Thy Tran, for trimming the manuscript's fat without forfeiting richness.

We are indebted to our wine consultant, Tim Patterson, for his discriminating palate and deep understanding of wine, food, and the synergies of the two. Tim put us back on track when we became sidetracked by certain wine regions and varietals, reminding us of those less well-known but equally intoxicating in their delights.

We are grateful to wineries and wine merchants too numerous to list for providing wine advice, sharing their personal favorites, and introducing us to delicious examples we might not have found on our own. A few among them are John DeGregory of Beringer Winery, Suzanne Janke of Château des Charmes, Sue Cottrell of Freemark Abbey, Inniskillin, Bruce Donsker of Van Der Heyden Vineyards, Paterno Imports, Roberta Klugman of the Livermore Valley Winegrowers Association, and the staffs of The Wine Experience in Broomfield, Colorado, The Sonoma Wine Shop, and Paul Marcus Wines and Vino! in Oakland, California.

We thank our agents Rebecca Staffel and Doe Coover for making the quintessential match: between Chronicle Books and us. We are immensely grateful to Bill LeBlond for sharing our excitement in the topic and for providing all manner of insight and support, and to everyone at Chronicle Books—including Brett McFadden, Jan Hughes, Doug Ogan, and Beth Steiner—for helping us realize our vision. In particular we thank Amy Treadwell for always knowing exactly what needed to happen next and for sharing sage advice along the way. Frankie Frakeny makes us hungry all over again with her lush photography, and she couldn't have done that without her talented stylist, Diane Gsell, and their many assistants; all were a joy to work with.

Although this book is a partnership in every way, we each have our own supports to thank. Jennie thanks her mentor and friend Flo Braker, with whom she exchanged many late-night emails and who always has a word of encouragement. Antonia Allegra offered sparks along the way, including asking Jennie to assist at *Appellation* magazine and nudging her to pursue a certificate program at the Cornell University School of Hotel Administration. A big hug to Mervyn Schacht, who always wanted his daughter to write a book with literary quotes opening the chapters and who conducted research to identify ones that hit the spot, and to Leatrice Schacht, for whom it is always time for dessert. A special thanks to Birdi for putting up with the odd hours of a baker-writer, a refrigerator perpetually overflowing with eggs and butter, and a house littered with empty (though often stylish) wine bottles.

Mary offers her appreciation to Toni Allegra and Flo Braker, as well, along with her colleagues at Cook Street School of Fine Cooking for their support and assistance with weaving a book into her busy life as a baking instructor. Bette Smith, wine director, kindly assisted in pairing wines with several of the desserts in the book. She is also grateful to those who have helped and inspired her along her path: Cathy Cochran-Lewis, Marcus Farbinger, Master Pastry Chef Albert Kumin, Roland Mesnier, Ewald Notter, and Charlie Trotter, as well as her loving partner, and her late husband, Michael Cech, for their enduring support.

To the many others we have failed to mention, please know that your enthusiasm and assistance are reflected in these pages and appreciated in our hearts.

What wond'rous life in this I lead!

Ripe apples drop about my head;

The luscious clusters of the vine

Upon my mouth do crush their wine;

The nectarine and curious peach,

Into my hands themselves do reach;

Stumbling on melons, as I pass,

Ensnar'd with flow'rs, I fall on grass.

— ANDREW MARVELL, "THE GARDEN"

INTRODUCTION

There is only one rule when it comes to pairing desserts and sweet wines: Eat what you like, drink what you enjoy with it. As with all matters of taste—music, clothing, friends—enjoyment of wine is much more a matter of personal preference than of scientific calculation. Nowhere is this truer than in the most indulgent portion of the meal: dessert. § This book invites you to learn more about what you like. We offer an overview of sweet wines and guidelines for matching them with desserts, then share recipes from delicate to decadent, each with detailed wine pairing notes. § We have two suggestions for getting started. First, sample, sample, sample. Fortunately, most dessert wines will keep well for a week or more after they have been opened. (The exceptions are vintage-dated reds, which are best consumed within a day or two of opening.) As you open and taste wines, you can keep several on hand. When you prepare a dessert, try it with several different wines. Observe how the dessert's flavors are enhanced or masked by the wine, and likewise, how the wine's character changes after a bite of the dessert. Try making several desserts, opening a few bottles of differing styles, inviting friends, and exploring the combinations together. § Our second suggestion is to get to know a local wine merchant. Wine buyers taste hundreds of wines to cull the offerings you find in their stores. A small wine shop is similar to a clothing boutique: Once you find one with selections you tend to like, you can count on them to carry others that mirror your taste. Don't be shy to chat with the proprietors. As they begin to know your preferences they can introduce you to new wines likely to be a good fit.

If you're wondering where good dessert wines come from, there's a simple answer: every place that produces wine. Sweet wines have been integral to wine production and consumption from day one. In fact, for most of wine-drinking history the sweet stuff has been the norm, dry wines the exception. § Contemporary sweet wines are mostly handcrafted in small batches. Fine dessert wines require far more time, work, and expense in the vineyard and in the cellar. For the winemaker, they are more a labor of love than a commodity. Travel anywhere with a climate hospitable to grapes and you'll likely find a fascinating local dessert wine. § With individual labels sometimes hard to find, a general sense of sweet wine styles makes easy work of identifying a suitable substitute. While current technologies make it possible to mimic almost any style in any region, there are certain broad regional patterns in dessert wine types, roughly corresponding to stages of wine history. § That wines originally were created sweet was unavoidable. Before the introduction of cultivated yeast strains in the nineteenth century (thank you, Louis Pasteur), it wasn't easy to convert all of the sugar in grapes to alcohol during fermentation. Some remained in the finished wine, leaving a sweet impression. Though perhaps inadvertent, this sweetness was held in high regard. Most legendary wines of antiquity were on the sticky side. Venice made a fortune for six centuries shipping Greece's sweet malvasia to Western Europe, where the British dubbed it "malmsey." Great Britain fought wars to control the port trade. In fact, the wine reputedly in longest continual production is a traditional honey-sweet one from Cyprus called Commandaria St. John, popularized by the Knights of St. John in

To take wine into our mouths is to savor a droplet of the river of human history.

— CLIFTON FADIMAN

the twelfth century and still produced from the same grape varietals today. Dry wines only assumed their air of superiority in the nineteenth century, and sweet wines continued to outsell them in California until the 1960s.

The popular enjoyment of wine, including sweet examples, began in Greece around 2000 BC. The islands in the Aegean were the original homeland of dessert wine styles that survive today, predecessors of Italian *vin santo* and that Cypriot Commandaria. The key to both these wines is using raisined grapes that produce a wine with some residual sugar and distinctive dried fruit flavors. Italy today is the center of this ancient style, which has echoes in certain dry red wine styles that incorporate a small amount of dried grapes, notably Valpolicella and Amarone. The Greeks also were early proponents of intentionally exposing sweet wine to heat and oxygen, an approach that later influenced fortified wines like sherry and Madeira.

Wine made from raisined grapes was the world's leading—perhaps only—consistent sweet wine style until late harvest wines emerged in Central Europe in the seventeenth century. Climate was critical. Allow grapes to stay on the vine in sunny Greece and, sooner or later, they will turn to raisins. But leave them hanging as winter approaches in continental Austria, Germany, or Hungary and they will either be attacked by the *Botrytis cinerea* mold, fondly dubbed the "noble rot," or they will freeze, producing *eiswein*. This late harvest style spread to Alsace in northeast France, which borders Germany and is very much influenced by its winemaking. Eventually the style took hold (with different grapes) in France's Sauternes region.

In Germany and Austria today, wines made from late harvested grapes are easy to identify once you learn the labeling code. Graded by the level of sugar in the grapes at harvest, the wines are called beerenauslese, German for fully ripened "selected berries," or trockenbeerenauslese, "dry selected berries" left on the vine until they have shriveled and dried from botrytis and evaporation. Many are rieslings, but you will also find furmint, scheurebe, sylvaner, and even chardonnay among them.

The sweetness level of Hungarian Tokaji is likewise indicated by the number of *puttonyos* (30-liter baskets) of paste made from botrytised grapes that went into the fermentation—anywhere from one to six. In France, the commune of origin gives the style away: sweet sémillon and sauvignon blanc come not only from Sauternes, but also from Barsac, Monbazillac, Cadillac, Loupiac, and neighboring towns. Similarly, in the Loire Valley, where the chenin blanc grape is the workhorse for wines sweet and dry, you will find not only Vouvray, but also Saumur, Anjou, Montlouis, and other area town names, as well as Quarts de Chaume and Bonnezeaux.

Late harvest winemaking has spread to every wine-growing region with a climate conducive to growing grapes. Australia has its share, but the highest concentration of quality late harvest wine producers in the New World is in the Finger Lakes region of upstate New York and across the Canadian border in Ontario. Both of these areas produce noteworthy ice wines in the German style.

The next wave of innovation came with fortification, a technique made possible by the availability of distilled grape spirits. Distillation for medicinal purposes dates back to the twelfth century, but commercial beverage applications first took off in the middle of the sixteenth century. By 1700, what we know today as port, sherry, and other fortified wines were in common production, with the original incentive being not so much flavor as the greater stability and longer shelf life the high alcohol levels afforded the wines.

Port from Portugal's Douro River Valley and sherry from Spain's Jerez and Sanlúcar regions are the best-known fortified styles, thanks largely to the eager British embrace of these wines in the eighteenth century. But alcohol-enhanced styles are common along the entire Mediterranean rim, especially in the south of France. This geographical pattern has prompted the half-serious observation that fortified wines are made in regions where it's too hot to drink them. The rule of thumb extends to California's Central Valley, home to most of the state's fortified wine producers, and Australia, another area of significant modern production.

The fortified category is large and complex, and there are great differences of opinion regarding the finer points of technique. For New World port-style winemakers, one dividing line is whether to add oak-aged brandy or neutral spirits to halt fermentation. The resulting differences in flavor can be dramatic. For sherry, where spirits are generally added after fermentation subsides, the degree of exposure to oxygen and the influence of various wild yeasts determine character.

In fortified French wines, *vin de liqueur* on the label means the extra alcohol was added before the onset of fermentation, keeping the grapes closest to their prefermented flavors, whereas *vin doux naturel* ("naturally sweet wine") indicates it was added later. Both retain some of the grapes' natural sweetness, and both are typically lower in alcohol than other fortified wines. Examples of vin doux naturel made from white grapes include Muscat de Beaumes-de-Venise, Muscat de Frontignan, and Muscat de

Rivesaltes. Reds, commonly made from grenache or a blend of grapes, include Banyuls and Maury. Pineau de Charantes is the most familiar example of vin de liqueur.

The final dessert style, sweet sparkling wine, is the most recent development of all. French wine with bubbles became a royal fad in the seventeenth century. Enterprising British merchants soon began putting it in heavier bottles with larger corks, but the bottle explosion rate remained unmanageably high well into the nineteenth century. Large-scale production of sweet sparklers only became possible after a series of technical breakthroughs: more precise measurement of sugar content, refrigeration, and the advent of filtration equipment.

Italy's Piedmont region leads the pack in this style with *frizzante* (lightly bubbly) Moscato d'Asti and the more robustly sparkling Asti, formerly known as Asti Spumante. Both are made from the muscat canelli grape. Most Champagne houses produce a small amount of *demi-sec* (sweet) and sometimes *doux* (very sweet) sparkling wine. Loire Valley producers offer sparklers made from chenin blanc labeled *demi-sec* or *moelleux* that range from *petillant*, or mildly bubbly, to full-tilt *mousseux*. Australia takes the cake with off-dry sparkling shiraz, bright red and frothy.

All you need to take the tour yourself is a map and a glass. And of course plenty of desserts to enjoy with the wines as you discover them.

— Tim Patterson

A DESSERT WINE PRIMER

Before we head off to the kitchen and wine rack, we offer this short lesson in sweet wines, their production, and how to pair them with desserts. To avoid getting bogged down in terminology, we have limited the jargon to the information we consider most important to your enjoyment of the recipes. § You may already have some idea of the wines you prefer with savory foods. You may look to complement flavors or textures, or sometimes contrast them for balance. Common wisdom dictates that white wines go best with light meats and most fish, for example, and red wines with earthier fare. There are basic rules to go by or, if you prefer, to break. Over time, wine enthusiasts grow comfortable adjusting the guidelines to suit their palates. § We are on shakier *terroir* at the end of the meal. When pairing desserts with sweet wines, we haven't much of a code to guide us. Although operating without an instruction manual can prove overwhelming, it also frees us of the burden of preconceived notions. No rules, no mistakes. § Desserts paired with wines are a luscious indulgence. They offer an extravagance for celebrating a special occasion or the inspiration for extending an evening with friends. Such unrivaled luxury should not feel like a test! § With this book, we set out on an adventure through territories both familiar and uncharted. We begin with basic information about how sweet wines get sweet, what choices are available, and a few simple guidelines to help you focus as you experiment. The rest of the learning curve is pure fun: nibbling and sipping various combinations until pairing desserts with wines becomes so familiar you can hardly remember when it seemed obscure.

Wine is a little like love; when the right one comes along, you know it.

— BOLLA WINES OF ITALY

why so sweet?

Dessert wines are made from many grape varietals in numerous styles. The one thing uniting them: They're sweet. How did they get that way?

Apart from the bargain-basement wines of our youth, most sweet wines do not depend on added sugar. Rather, the natural sugar in the grapes is concentrated, or fermentation is halted before all the sugar is converted to alcohol, or a combination of the two.

There are a number of ways to concentrate the natural sugar in grapes destined for sweet wines. The principal methods are allowing the grapes to become very ripe on the vine, drying the grapes, and freezing them. Leaving them to be attacked by a wine-friendly fungus can further concentrate sugar and flavor.

late harvest white wines

To create late harvest wines, winemakers leave grapes on the vine long after grapes for dry wines have been harvested. With continued ripening, the grapes become extraordinarily sweet. The grower monitors sugar levels in the grapes, usually measured in degrees Brix, until they reach the optimal level. Grapes for sweet wines are left on the vine until they reach 30 to as much as 65 degrees Brix. By comparison, table grapes are picked at about 15 degrees Brix and grapes for dry wines at about 20 to 25. Late harvest wines often state the degrees Brix at harvest on the label, a clue to the grapes' ripeness.

Grape juice is turned into wine by fermentation—the breakdown of sugar by yeasts into alcohol and carbon dioxide. By knowing the sweetness of the grapes, the winemaker can estimate the potential alcohol level of the wine they will produce. Depending on wine-making techniques and conditions, the amount of

sugar converted yields roughly half that percentage of alcohol. In other words, grapes picked at 24 degrees Brix can be fully fermented into a wine with about 12 percent alcohol. In this case, all of the sugar has been used up in the fermentation process, so the wine will be dry.

When grapes are picked super-ripe, the picture changes. High sugar content and rising alcohol levels will bring fermentation to a grinding halt before the yeasts have a chance to convert all the sugar into alcohol. The remaining sugar, called residual sugar, gives dessert wines their distinctive sweetness. Residual sugar levels of 10 to 30 percent are common in late harvest wines.

Late harvest white wines are made from many grape varietals. Some of the most common are riesling, sauvignon blanc, sémillon, chenin blanc, and gewürztraminer. Ranging from lightly sweet to intensely so, they can have flavors of peach, apricot, apple, pear, pineapple, and other tropical fruits, as well as flowers, spice, vanilla, butter, honey, caramel, and musk.

wines made from dried grapes

Grapes may also be concentrated by drying. Under the right conditions, grapes left on the vine will turn to raisins. Loss of water in the grapes means more concentrated sugar and flavor. Grapes may be picked and then dried on straw mats to achieve the same effect. These wines typically taste of raisins and other dried fruit and sometimes nuts. If you've ever dipped your biscotti into a glass of *vin santo*, you are familiar with a common version of this style.

ice wines

A third way to make wines sweet is by allowing the grapes to freeze. In very cold climates, grapes may be left on the vines late into the winter and harvested only after they are frozen. The water inside the grapes freezes and clings later to the press, separating it from the sweet nectar collected for wine making. The resulting wines are called *eisweins* in Germany and Austria, icewines in Canada, and ice wines in the United States.

Ice wines are a risky and expensive business. A whole crop can be lost if the conditions aren't right, and only a small amount of juice is collected from the grapes. But the resulting wine is well worth the effort: made well, ice wines can be intensely sweet, brimming with complex flavors of tropical fruit, peach, dried apricot, melon, and sometimes floral or honeyed flavors. Some winemakers in warmer climates make icebox wines, mimicking the effect by freezing the grapes after harvest. In cold climates, winemakers often use riesling grapes to make ice wines. Some hybrid grapes, such as the vidal varietal used in Canada's Niagara Peninsula, also appear in ice wines.

noble rot

Whatever the method of evaporation and concentration, grapes left late on the vine may be attacked by the fungus *Botrytis cinerea*, which causes grapes to shrivel and lose moisture. If you've ever seen a bunch of grapes consumed by botrytis, you'd be hard-pressed to believe such ugly grapes could make such an exquisite wine.

The shriveling of the grapes further concentrates the grapes' sugar and acid for a sweet, powerful aromatic wine with enough acid to keep it from tasting cloying. Botrytis sets into action other chemical changes that add to the wine's complexity, giving the resulting wines a creamy texture in the mouth and deep, often earthy flavors of dried fruit, honey, butterscotch, and nuts.

Botrytised wines can be quite expensive because harvesters pick each individual grape by hand as it reaches the optimal stage of ripeness and dehydration. The fungus is fickle. It doesn't come every year, and not all grapes in a vineyard—or even in a single bunch of grapes—will be consumed by it. Wine-makers occasionally spray grapes with botrytis after harvest to develop the characteristic and highly prized flavors.

Varietals commonly affected by botrytis include chenin blanc, furmint, muscadelle, muscat, riesling, sauvignon blanc, and sémillon. Probably the best-known botrytised wines are made in Bordeaux's Sauternes regions; the most prized are produced by Chateau d'Yquem. Many German and Austrian sweet wines are kissed by botrytis, as is Hungarian Tokaji. *Aszú* is the Hungarian term for botrytised grapes.

stopping fermentation

Sometimes a winemaker will halt fermentation before the yeasts have converted all the sugar from the grapes into alcohol, capturing some of the grapes' natural sweetness in the finished wine.

The most common method for stopping fermentation is by fortifying the wine with brandy or neutral spirits distilled from grapes. The influx of alcohol makes the wine inhospitable to yeast and quickly stops fermentation; most yeasts die once the wine's alcohol level reaches 13 to 15 percent. Fortification provides the finished wine sufficient alcohol without using up all the grapes' sugar. Chilling and filtration are also used to halt fermentation.

Port, sherry, and Madeira are common examples of fortified wines. In France and Australia, muscat is often made in a fortified style. A variety of red wine grapes are fortified to make nontraditional ports. Fortified wines typically have higher alcohol levels than their late harvested cousins. Flavor profiles vary according to the grapes used. Port flavors can range from currants or berries to chocolate. Sherry tends toward nutty flavors of almond, walnut, and hazelnut. Madeira, named for the Portuguese island of the same moniker, gets its characteristic flavors of dark caramel, toasted nuts, and wood—with a pleasant hint of bitterness—from heat and oxidization during winemaking. The malvasia (malmsey) grape is used to make the sweetest, most intense Madeira.

name that port

Traditional ports are fortified wines made in Portugal's Douro Valley and shipped from Oporto, from whence they get their name. Port is made from a large number of native varietals and comes in several styles. *Ruby port* is the youngest and fruitiest of the bunch, and generally the least expensive. Named for its color, *tawny port* is blended from multiple vintages and aged in wood from 10 to 40 years. *Vintage port* is made using grapes from a single vintage only in years when quality dictates that a vintage be declared. Aged only briefly before bottling, it is designed to mature in the bottle. *Late bottled vintage port* is made from a single vintage, though not a declared vintage. It is aged in wood for up to 6 years and is ready to drink once bottled. *Colheita port* is a single vintage tawny port aged in wood for at least 7 years. *Single-quinta port* is produced using grapes from a single wine estate.

sparkling sweet wines

Some sweet wines are made in a sparkling style. A very charming example is the Moscato d'Asti of Italy's Piedmont region. Produced from the moscato bianco grape (also known as muscat canelli), the wine typically has a floral aroma and just a prickle of effervescence. Moscato wines often taste of green grape, pear, or apple. Low in alcohol, they leave a clean, refreshing impression and are wonderful served chilled with light desserts highlighting fresh fruit.

The fizz comes from carbon dioxide, a natural by-product of fermentation, which is often captured by chilling. Wines can also sparkle from a secondary fermentation, induced either in steel tanks or in the bottle.

late harvest red wines

Most red grapes made in sweet styles are fortified. There are two reasons for this. First, the demand for dry red wines consumes most of the red grape harvest. Second, red grapes are more susceptible to molds and other difficulties, making late harvesting a precarious proposition. While botrytis can turn white wine grapes into liquid gold, the same fungus will render most red wine grapes unusable. A safer approach is to pick red grapes ripe, then fortify the wine to raise its alcohol level and retain some residual sugar. Still, a few winemakers take the risk of leaving grapes on the vine late into the season in the manner of late harvest white wines, and their results can be alluring.

an ABC of wine designations

Understanding a few key terms can help you to decipher wine labels from the major sweet wine-producing countries. The French classify their best wines as AOC (appellation of controlled origin) or AC. These wines meet strict criteria for the vineyard's location, varietals included and their yields, winemaking practices employed, and the alcohol content and taste of the finished wine. The equivalent designations in neighboring countries are DO (denomination of origin) in Spain and DOC (controlled denomination of origin) in Italy and Portugal. Italy adds a higher designation, DOCG (controlled and guaranteed denomination of origin), which only selected areas are permitted to use.

In the German system, wines are classified in six QmP (*Qualitätswein mit Prädikat*, roughly translated "quality wine with distinction") subcategories, from lowest to highest sugar level at harvest. QmP wines must be from a defined district (appellation), estate bottled, and produced without added sugar. Grapes at the two highest levels (beerenauslese and trocken-beerenauslese) are commonly affected by botrytis and make the sweetest, most full-bodied, intensely flavored wines. Grapes for eisweins must be picked at one of these two highest levels.

The American AVA (American Viticultural Area) system classifies wine by appellation; 85 percent of the grapes must be grown within the AVA to qualify for the designation. The Vintners Quality Alliance (VQA) is the Canadian system for designating and labeling wines, and the highest level is the Designated Viticultural Area (DVA). VQA wines made from grapes picked at the highest sugar levels—from frozen grapes—are designated icewines.

Pairing Desserts with Sweet Wines

The only way to really know sweet wines is to try them, alone and in combination with desserts. When pairing wines with desserts, you will want to take into consideration their weight or richness as well as their flavors. Wines are often described as being light- or full-bodied. Alcohol and sugar levels are the chief contributors to a wine's weight. High sugar levels in dessert wines give them more body than the lightest dry wines. On the light end of the spectrum, a young riesling will feel something like apple juice in the mouth. At the other end, some botrytised wines, ice wines, and fortified wines may be almost as thick as maple syrup.

Pairing Guidelines

We offer these rules of thumb to get you started

GUIDELINE	EXAMPLES
Pair desserts with wines that are sweeter than the dessert. If you sample a sweet dessert and then sip a wine that is less sweet, the wine will suddenly taste flat or sour.	Enjoy lightly sweetened fresh fruit with a gently sweet Moscato d'Asti. Try sticky-sweet caramel with a super-sweet beerenauslese or trockenbeerenauslese.
Match the weight of the wine to the richness of dessert.	Pair lighter-bodied wines having little or no oak and no botrytis with fresh fruit desserts—a young late harvest gewürztraminer with poached apricots, for example, or a Brachetto d'Acqui with red fruits. Late harvest whites with a little more body, perhaps aged in oak, pair nicely with caramel and buttery flavors. The most full-bodied whites—ice wines and botrytised wines—are great companions to rich dairy desserts like crème brûlée.
Carbonation makes wines versatile and refreshing. Sweet sparkling wines are restrained enough to avoid overwhelming lighter desserts, while providing a welcome palate cleanser for richer sweets.	A sparkling muscat is perfection with a delicate poached peach, while a sparkling Vouvray can keep a dense cheesecake from becoming overwhelming.
Fortified wines, with their typically higher alcohol levels, stand up well to rich desserts with deep flavors of nuts, caramel, and chocolate.	Sherry almost always pairs well with nuts. The tannin in port and port-style wines is a lovely match with chocolate.
Look to complement, marry, or gently contrast the dessert's flavors with the wine.	A lively wine with citrus notes, perhaps a late harvest riesling, will enliven a dessert that calls out for a squeeze of lemon. The caramel flavors in Madeira make it a welcome companion to a tarte Tatin.
Don't make your wine and dessert fight for attention. If the wine is complex, show it off with a simpler dessert. To highlight a dessert with many elements or flavors, choose a more straightforward wine.	Save your Chateau d'Yquem for sipping with only the very simplest sweets.

Pairing Suggestions

This chart sorts out the major dessert wine styles, providing a few examples of each and suggesting matches that are typically compatible with each style. We hope you will use this chart to record your own favorite pairings as you explore the endless combinations of desserts and wines.

WINE STYLE	EXAMPLES	DESSERT FLAVORS												
		PEACH, NECTARINE & APRICOT	CHERRY & PLUM	BERRIES	CITRUS	APPLE, PEAR & QUINCE	ROASTED & STEWED FRUITS	TROPICAL FRUITS	DRIED FRUITS	BUTTER, CREAM & CUSTARD	CARAMEL, HONEY & BUTTERSCOTCH	SPICE	TOASTED NUTS	CHOCOLATE
Sparkling wines	Asti and Moscato d'Asti Brachetto d'Acqui Demi-sec Champagne Sparkling Vouvray	✓	✓	✓	✓	✓		✓		✓	✓			
Fresh, late harvest whites with little or no oak or botrytis	Late harvest riesling, sauvignon blanc, sémillon, chenin blanc, gewürztraminer Vouvray	✓		✓	✓	✓	✓					✓		
Aged white wines	Late harvest riesling, sauvignon blanc, sémillon Loire Valley chenin-blancs Some Sauternes and neighboring communes	✓			✓	✓	✓	✓	✓	✓	✓			
Botrytised wines	Beerenauslese and trockenbeerenauslese Sauternes and neighboring communes Some ice wines Tokaji				✓	✓	✓	✓	✓	✓	✓	✓	✓	
Ice wines	Canadian icewines German and Austrian eisweins Ice wines from the Finger Lakes region	✓			✓	✓	✓	✓	✓	✓	✓			

		DESSERT FLAVORS												
WINE STYLE	EXAMPLES	PEACH, NECTARINE & APRICOT	CHERRY & PLUM	BERRIES	CITRUS	APPLE, PEAR & QUINCE	ROASTED & STEWED FRUITS	TROPICAL FRUITS	DRIED FRUITS	BUTTER, CREAM & CUSTARD	CARAMEL, HONEY & BUTTERSCOTCH	SPICE	TOASTED NUTS	CHOCOLATE
Raisined wines	*Passito* *Vin de paille* *Vin santo*		✓						✓		✓	✓	✓	
Light- and medium-bodied red wines	*Banyuls* *Black muscat* *Brachetto d'Acqui* *Dulce monastrell* *Maury* *Ruby port*		✓	✓									✓	✓
Fortified wines	*Fortified Australian and French muscats* *Port (tawny, LBV, vintage)* *Port-style wines from nontraditional grapes*		✓	✓					✓		✓	✓	✓	✓
Oxidized wines	*Madeira* *Sherry*									✓	✓	✓	✓	✓

Write in a favorite wine and check your preferred pairings below.

The right equipment for the job; confidence in technique; and the selection, accurate measurement, and optimal temperature of ingredients are the baker's essential tools for turning out first-rate desserts every time.

INGREDIENTS

In most cases, room-temperature ingredients (68 to 75 degrees F) produce the lightest, airiest cakes by allowing for the optimal emulsification of ingredients and the incorporation of extra air into the batter. Ingredients for flaky pastry are an exception. Here, cold butter and flour produce the optimal result.

It will take 30 to 60 minutes for refrigerated ingredients to come to room temperature on the counter, depending on the density of the ingredients and the temperatures of both your refrigerator and kitchen. Tips for quickly bringing butter and eggs to room temperature follow.

almond paste

This paste of finely ground, sweetened almonds is found in seven-ounce tubes in the baking section of most supermarkets or in bulk in upscale groceries, health food stores, and cake-decorating supply shops. A commonly available brand is Odense. Marzipan is softer and sweeter, and does not always make a good substitute. Tightly wrap leftover bulk almond paste in aluminum foil and store it in an airtight container at room temperature.

Occasionally, the sugar in an opened package of almond paste may crystallize, forming a crust or hardening the paste. To soften it, place the unwrapped roll in a resealable plastic bag or airtight container with a slice or two of bread or a couple of apple slices. Seal tightly and leave at room temperature several hours or overnight.

To make an apple pie from scratch, you must first invent the universe.

— CARL SAGAN

butter

We recommend using high-quality butter for recipes where butter is a major ingredient. Unless specified, we use unsalted butter as it provides the freshest flavor and allows for greater control of a recipe's salt level.

We often call for butter to be softened to room temperature or used while still cold. Butter at room temperature should be soft enough to bend easily without either breaking or falling apart. Cold butter, the key to flaky pastry, should come directly from the refrigerator and should be very firm but not frozen.

To soften cold butter quickly, microwave the wrapped butter on a small plate for about 20 seconds at medium power. (If the butter is frozen, start out with the defrost setting for one minute.) Continue to microwave in 10-second increments, turning the butter each time, until it is just soft and pliable but not at all melted. Cutting cold butter in thin slices and placing them in a single layer around the inside surface of a mixing bowl will also accelerate softening.

Some of the brands we have used and like that are widely available are European-Style Butter from Straus Family Creamery, Land O'Lakes, Beurre President Gastronomique, Kerrygold, and Plugrá.

cream

Carrageenan, monoglycerides, and diglycerides are sometimes added to produce more volume or to stabilize cream when whipped. Especially for crème brûlée and other desserts that will need to set, purchase cream without additives or emulsifiers.

Our recipes generally call for whipping cream, which contains 30 to 36 percent butterfat. At 36 to 40 percent butterfat, heavy whipping cream contributes more body. We prefer pasteurized cream over ultra-pasteurized for its superior dairy flavor and best whipping volume.

eggs

For the best flavor and volume, use eggs within the freshness date stamped on the carton. To warm refrigerated eggs quickly to room temperature, submerge them in a bowl of warm (not hot) water for a few minutes until they no longer feel chilly to the touch. Keep in mind that eggs separate more easily when cold but rise to a greater volume when beaten at room temperature. Separate cold eggs before beginning the recipe, and then leave them at room temperature, tightly covered, until you need them.

When beating egg whites for a meringue, use an impeccably clean bowl and beater to prevent any fat from impeding the whites' rise to maximum volume. Whip in superfine sugar, adding it very slowly to ensure that it dissolves completely.

For recipes that use only egg whites, look for the pasteurized liquid egg whites available in many supermarkets. Substitute two tablespoons of liquid egg white for each large egg white.

To store leftover egg whites, refrigerate them for up to four days or freeze for up to one year. Use a tightly sealed container, and be sure to label it with the date and number of whites. Thaw frozen whites overnight in the refrigerator and use as you would fresh ones. For easier measuring, freeze individual whites in separate compartments of an ice cube tray and transfer to a freezer bag once frozen.

Cover leftover egg yolks with a little water and refrigerate in an airtight container. (Pour off water before using.) Yolks can be frozen for up to a year, but they require special care because they tend to thicken and become gelatinous. To slow the process, whisk ⅛ teaspoon salt or 1½ teaspoons sugar into ¼ cup of yolks (about 4 large yolks). Freeze in an airtight container labeled with the date, number of yolks, and whether you added salt or sugar.

flour

Unless otherwise stated, the recipes assume unbleached all-purpose flour. Flour labeled "bread flour" or "best for bread" has too much protein for most recipes in this book. Do not substitute self-rising flours, which have other ingredients added. Store flour in the freezer to maintain freshness and to keep pastry dough cold as you mix it.

Cake flour, which has less protein than all-purpose flour, assures a light, tender crumb in delicate desserts. Most supermarkets stock it (look for Pillsbury's Softasilk), but in a pinch, you can substitute 1 cup minus 2 tablespoons all-purpose flour for every 1 cup of cake flour in a recipe. Use this substitution advisedly as it may result in a heavier or denser cake.

gelatin

Gelatin is commonly sold in a box of small packets, each holding ¼ ounce or about 2½ teaspoons of unflavored powder. Quantities in the packets vary slightly, so always measure carefully—small differences can turn a dessert from too loose to perfectly set to rubbery.

Soften gelatin by sprinkling it evenly over cold water or liquid from the recipe and letting it stand about five minutes undisturbed; stirring at this point will make it clump. Add the softened gelatin to a warm liquid and stir for at least a minute to thoroughly dissolve. It should be completely smooth, with no graininess.

When heating a liquid to be mixed with gelatin, or heating the softened gelatin, do not allow it to boil. Intense heat will weaken the gelatin's ability to set and may cause some of the gelatin to separate out in a clear layer. A warm temperature (110 to 130 degrees F) is all that's needed to dissolve the gelatin.

salt

We recommend fine sea salt for its cleaner taste and its ability to dissolve more readily than regular table salt. Kosher salt will generally work well, but its coarser grains may not dissolve completely in some recipes. To use kosher salt, substitute 1½ times the quantity specified in the recipe (for example, ¾ teaspoon kosher salt for ½ teaspoon fine sea salt).

sugar

Sugar can be derived from sugarcane or sugar beets. We recommend sugar labeled as pure cane sugar, as beet sugar does not always produce a reliable result. The smaller grain size of superfine sugar helps it dissolve more quickly and easily when making meringue or when beating sugar into a batter. Baker's sugar has a grain size between standard granulated and superfine sugar. You can substitute an equal quantity of baker's or superfine sugar for granulated sugar in the recipes in this book. Powdered sugar helps create a sandy texture in certain crusts and cookies, and is perfect for sifting over desserts. We recommend against substituting powdered sugar for granulated or vice versa in recipes.

vanilla

Select pure vanilla extract without artificial flavoring. We use whole vanilla beans where possible for truest vanilla flavor. Bourbon vanilla has an earthy-sweet flavor that complements, but doesn't overwhelm, other flavors in wines and desserts. Tahitian vanilla is fruity, floral, and intensely aromatic. Fresh beans will be pliable and moist. Store the beans, tightly wrapped in plastic, in an airtight jar in a cool, dark place for up to six months. The beans may be rinsed well after using, dried, and stored the same way. After most of the flavor has been extracted, place the beans in a jar of granulated sugar, which will be enhanced by their delicate flavor.

baking sheets

When we specify a baking sheet, we generally mean a 17-by-12-inch rimmed pan. We prefer heavy aluminum pans, which have less of a tendency to buckle. Watch carefully for browning when using pans with a dark finish.

cake pans

Baking pans with a dark finish can cause cakes to brown too quickly and form a thick, dark crust. For the most tender cakes, use light-colored, shiny pans of substantial weight. For 8- and 9-inch round pans, the recipes assume the pans are at least 2 inches deep.

glass baking pans

Glass conducts and retains heat well. Except where noted, we recommend metal pans. If you bake with glass pans, reduce the oven temperature by 25 degrees F.

pie pans

For pie pans, we recommend darker pans, whether uncoated or nonstick. These pans absorb more heat than lighter colored pans, creating crusts that are especially flaky or crumbly. Glass pie pans allow you to see how the crust is browning on the bottom.

ramekins

Ramekins and ceramic baking dishes are excellent for baking custards and other desserts. With the wide range of sizes, shapes, and colors available, they double as decorative serving dishes. To measure the capacity of a ramekin, fill it with water and then pour the water into a measuring cup. An 8-ounce ramekin will hold 1 cup of water; a 6-ounce one will hold ¾ cup. With custards and liquidy batters, you will generally want to leave ¼ inch of space at the top to avoid spills.

tart and tartlet pans

We recommend tart pans with removable bottoms for easy release of finished tarts. To remove the ring, balance the pan over a glass or bowl with a diameter smaller than the pan and let the ring drop away. Leave the tart on the base for serving, or use a wide spatula or a rimless baking sheet to transfer the tart to a serving platter.

Tart pans come in a wide range of sizes and include both rectangular and circular shapes. Most recipes in this book specify either a 9- or 10-inch round tart pan or 4-inch tartlet pans. Nonstick coatings are unnecessary when using tart pans for recipes with a buttery crust.

electric mixers and their attachments

A standing mixer, with its paddle and whisk attachments, is invaluable for creaming, whipping air into ingredients, and mixing over long periods of time. If you do not have a standing mixer, use a handheld electric mixer. We have noted tasks that can be accomplished in a food processor. A food processor is not a good substitute for recipes where the incorporation of air is important for a light result.

graters and rasps

Modeled after a woodworker's rasp, Microplane graters and zesters make easy work of a number of cooking tasks, from grating chocolate to zesting lemons. We love them for grating fluffy piles of fine zest from the outer rind of citrus fruits while avoiding the bitter pith beneath.

palette knives, offset spatulas, and bench scrapers

These flat metal spatulas in a wide range of sizes are useful for spreading batters in pans and for sliding under cookies and pastries to loosen or move them. Offset spatulas are the optimal tool for filling and icing cakes and for lifting a slice of pie or tart. Look for a stainless-steel blade for flexibility and a molded polypropylene handle with a good grip. A bench scraper with a stainless-steel blade and a molded or wood handle is useful for moving pastry as you roll it, for gathering chopped nuts from a cutting board, and for scraping a flat surface to clear away flour or sticky dough bits.

pastry bags

We like the plastic, disposable pastry bags commonly available in cookware stores. You can see what's inside the clear bags, and they are easily cleaned or discarded, avoiding crossover of flavors from previously used ingredients. The bags can be cut to fit round or decorative tips when needed. If you do not have a pastry bag, scoop the mixture into a resealable plastic bag. Gently press the air out of the bag and seal it. Taking care not to spill the contents, snip a small opening in a bottom corner of the bag and proceed as described in the recipe.

rolling pins

Most people find it easiest to roll dough to an even thickness using the traditional wooden rolling pin with handles and ball bearings. The wood holds a dusting of flour in place to avoid sticking. Marble pins add weight and keep pastry cool. Long, tapered wood rolling pins are light and easy to use, though they may make it more difficult to roll dough evenly.

saucepans

Certain metals react more easily with acidic ingredients, creating metallic and other off flavors and colors in the finished dessert. When we specify a nonreactive saucepan, we suggest a pan made of stainless steel or anodized aluminum, or one coated with a nonreactive lining such as the ceramic coating found on some cast-iron cookware. Avoid aluminum pans that are not anodized as well as cast-iron and copper pans that are not coated, as they react easily with citrus juices, wine, and other acidic ingredients.

silicone baking mats and parchment paper

Easy to clean and reuse, silicone baking mats make excellent stick-resistant pan liners. These mats are especially useful for candies, wafers, and very thin cookies, which peel off of the mats much more easily than from other nonstick surfaces.

Parchment paper is also convenient and effective. Parchment can be purchased in rolls, sheets for lining baking pans, and convenient rounds to fit cake pans in a variety of sizes.

Silicone mats and parchment paper can generally be used interchangeably. However, take care when using paper labeled "super parchment." This extremely slick, reusable parchment can cause problems with certain batters, which spread too thin or slip off the paper. We do not recommend waxed paper for most oven uses, as the wax coating can melt or smoke in the oven.

spatulas

A heat-resistant spatula is indispensable for scraping bowls and stirring ingredients as they are heated, especially in custards and sauces where air added by a whisk is not desirable. They also help prevent curdling and scorching by scraping clean the bottom and sides of the bowl or pot.

whisks

Large balloon whisks incorporate air into ingredients quickly and effectively. Flat whisks are useful for reaching the corners of a saucepan as you stir and cook. Use a plastic or coated whisk with nonstick cookware.

wine glasses

Most wine glasses taper up from a broad bowl, collecting the wine's complex aromas and delivering them to your nose as you drink. Some glassmakers produce wine glasses designed for specific varietals —Sauternes, sparkling wines, and fortified wines among them. While these can be quite elegant and may enhance the wine experience, a simple wine glass will serve the purpose.

Select stemmed glasses that hold six to eight ounces of wine. Although dessert wines are typically served in small portions of one to three ounces, the glass should be large enough for swirling. The small serving will be lost in an oversized glass, while tiny cordial glasses won't provide a full sensory experience.

Plain, clear stemware does the best job of showcasing wine, and thin-walled glasses tend to deliver wine to the mouth most gracefully. Hold the glass by the stem or base to prevent your hand from warming the wine or leaving smudges that obscure it. Wash and rinse glassware thoroughly to avoid residual flavors and aromas.

baking basics

Always begin by carefully reading the recipe to avoid any surprises. Baking relies on careful measurement of ingredients and close attention to technique. While extra herbs and garlic may deepen the flavor of a soup, too much flour can make the difference between a light, airy cake and something better suited for a hockey rink. Familiarizing yourself with the recipe, preparing the equipment, and measuring the ingredients first will help you to follow the recipe more easily.

creating a water bath

To insulate delicate custards and cheesecakes against the oven's harsh, drying heat, create a water bath by nesting the pans or molds inside a larger pan. Lining the outer pan with a folded tea towel helps to avoid splashing as you pour hot water into the outer pan, prevents the pans from sliding, and further insulates the dessert.

cutting fruits

CITRUS: To cut oranges and other citrus into decorative segments, cut a thin slice off the top and bottom of the fruit and place it cut-side down on a cutting board. With a sharp, thin-bladed knife, cut wide strips of peel from top to bottom. Make your way around the orange, being sure to cut away the white pith along with the rind. Working over a bowl to catch its juices, pick up the peeled fruit and cut against one of the membranes toward the center to separate a segment of fruit from the membrane. Now turn the knife to angle it slightly and drag the blade against the membrane on the other side of the segment to release it. Repeat until all the segments have been removed. You may have to cut along both sides of the membrane to remove some of the segments. Finally, squeeze the remaining juice from the membranes over the segments and discard the membranes.

MANGO: There are two basic ways to peel and cut a mango. To chop a mango into cubes, place the mango, skin still on, on a cutting board on one of its narrow sides. Use a sharp paring knife to cut away the cheeks from both flat sides of the pit. Place one of the cheeks skin-side down on the board and cut a crosshatch pattern into the flesh, taking care not to cut through the skin. Pull the two farthest ends back to invert the mango; the cubes will pop out in relief. Use a sharp knife to cut the flesh from the skin.

To peel a mango, place the fruit on a cutting board on one of its narrow sides and use a sharp paring knife to remove the skin. With a large, sharp knife, cut away the cheeks from both flat sides of the pit. To slice the fruit, use a mandoline or place the mango pieces flat-side down and slice them as thinly as possible with a sharp knife. To julienne, arrange the slices in neat stacks and cut them crosswise.

POMEGRANATE: To remove seeds from a pomegranate, first don an apron—pomegranate juice stains! The seeds consist of a small, crunchy white pit surrounded by juicy red flesh; the whole seed is edible. Score the fruit from top to bottom in about five places, then break it apart at the score marks. Hold one section over a bowl placed in the sink and push the seeds out with your fingers. Pull away and discard membranes, extraneous fibers, and damaged seeds. Pour cold water over the seeds in the bowl. Most of the remaining fibers will float and can be easily removed. Drain the seeds and refrigerate them in a tightly covered container.

judging doneness

The cooking and baking times provided in the recipes are guidelines. There are so many variables affecting cooking and baking times, we cannot possibly account for them all. Wherever possible, we include indicators of doneness to help you know what to look for. We recommend checking for the desired color and texture at least five minutes before the suggested time, then gauging the additional time needed. Use all your senses and trust your instincts.

maintaining oven temperature

If you are uncertain whether your oven is well calibrated, purchase an oven thermometer. They are often more reliable than the oven's internal thermometer. Even small variations in temperature and baking time can make a big difference between a dessert that is moist and tender, or dry and tough.

For even baking, rotate pans halfway through the suggested baking time, front to back and, if using two racks simultaneously, top to bottom. If a dessert is browning too quickly before it is done, drape a piece of foil over the top or reduce the oven temperature by 25 degrees.

measuring flour

Always measure flour before sifting unless otherwise indicated. Aerate flour before measuring by scooping the flour with a spoon or measuring cup until it is fluffy. Using a flat-topped measuring cup (save your glass measures for wet ingredients), spoon the flour into the cup until it is heaped over the top, then draw the back of a knife across the top to even it.

melting chocolate

Melt chocolate in a double boiler over, but not touching, simmering water and stir it with a spatula just until smooth. Avoid scorching, which can make the chocolate bitter, or moisture, which can cause it to seize and clump.

To melt chocolate in a microwave oven, heat the coarsely chopped chocolate in an uncovered microwave-safe glass bowl at medium (50 percent) power for one minute. Stir with a rubber spatula; the chocolate may retain its shape even after it is melted. Continue to microwave, stirring every 30 seconds after the first minute to distribute the heat and melt any small pieces. The time needed to melt the chocolate will depend on your microwave's wattage, the size and shape of your bowl, the type and quantity of chocolate, and how coarsely it is chopped.

preparing cake pans

Always carefully follow directions for preparing pans. When buttering pans, coat them generously and evenly to reduce sticking. Use all-purpose flour to coat pans; cake flour tends to clump. Knock the pan against the side of the sink to tap out excess flour. In many recipes, we suggest lining the bottom of the pan with parchment paper as an extra safeguard against sticking.

whipping cream

To achieve the greatest volume and to prevent inadvertently making butter, always start with very cold cream, bowl, and beaters. Place the bowl and beaters in the refrigerator at least 10 minutes before whipping the cream.

Cream may be whipped to soft, medium, or firm peaks. Soft peaks look like soft, billowy clouds. Medium peaks hold their shape and lose a bit of the sheen you see on soft peaks. Stiff or firm peaks will hold their shape well but will not be broken and separated. For whipped cream that will be served as a topping, we recommend medium peaks, which feel creamy and smooth in the mouth.

whipping egg whites

Recipes specify beating whites to soft, medium, or firm peaks. At the soft peak stage, when you lift the beaters you will see a rounded peak that doesn't hold its shape. At medium peaks, the whites will look smooth and a little shiny. The peaks will hold their shape well, but their tips will curve over gently when you lift the beaters. They will not be altogether stiff and will never appear dry or begin to separate. Firm peaks will stand straight up at attention when you lift the beaters but should never be stiff or dry. It is all too easy to go from this stage to overbeaten whites, which will look separated and have the appearance of plastic foam.

Unless otherwise specified, we recommend beating egg whites to medium peaks. At this stage, the whites are easier to fold into doughs and do a better job of holding the air you have taken such care to beat into them. Stiff whites can collapse, and can make cakes tough with their overdeveloped proteins.

working with pastry dough

Several of the pastry crusts in this book include sugar and softened butter. While this type of pastry requires special care, it results in a rich and tender crust that holds up well to a variety of fillings. Once you've mastered it, you will be rewarded with a distinctive crust that delivers outstanding texture and flavor.

The following tips will make preparing pastry easy as pie:

* Chill the dough before rolling, then work quickly and handle the dough as little as possible to keep it cool.

* After removing the chilled dough from the refrigerator, knead it two to four times, just until it is the consistency of firm sculpting clay. You are looking to integrate the ingredients to ease handling and to help prevent the pastry from tearing or falling apart. This also helps to warm it just slightly, making it easier to roll. But take care—if the dough becomes too warm and difficult to work with, return it to the refrigerator to chill again.

* As you roll the dough, keep the work surface, the top of the dough, and the rolling pin well floured. Pick up and turn the dough frequently, sprinkling a little flour beneath it to prevent sticking. A bench scraper or large metal spatula is invaluable for keeping the pastry mobile.

* Since this rich dough tends to tear and fall apart if folded, the best way to transfer it to the pan is by using a thin, rimless baking sheet, lightly dusted with flour, as a large spatula. Be sure to center the dough before pressing it evenly into the bottom and sides of the pan. To trim the edge, press your rolling pin firmly over the top of the pan.

* If your pastry tears or falls apart despite following these tips, fear not. Lay it into the pan as best you can, then use dough scraps to patch together any tears or spaces. A bit of water can help to adhere the dough and seal cracks. Though finicky, this type of dough is easily manipulated and very forgiving.

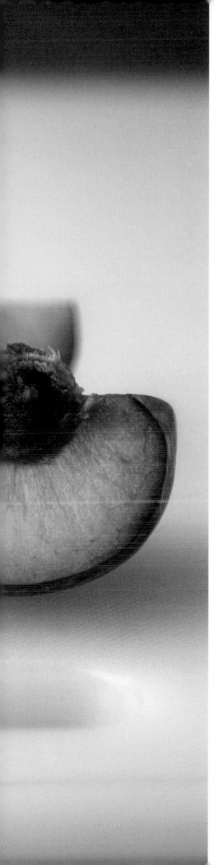

STONE FRUITS

Poised over the kitchen basin, you sink your teeth into the rosy fuzz of a peach so juicy the nectar runs off your chin. Summer has arrived! Peaches, plums, nectarines, apricots, pluots, cherries—these fruits with a pit at the center are the classic symbol of summer. § Because the flavors of stone fruits are so prevalent in white wines, desserts made with these fruits are among the most fun to match. Relatively gentle, delicate dessert wines harmonize with the nuances typical of stone fruits without overpowering them. A young German riesling or Alsatian late harvest pinot gris would be a natural match, as would a dance-on-your-tongue sparkler such as an Asti, Moscato d'Asti, or Brachetto. Many moderate to sweet late harvest whites enhance the flavor of these desserts. Ice wines can produce peach and nectarine tones. So long as they are not too heavy or syrupy sweet, malvasia bianca and white and orange muscats, both fortified and not, offer aromatic matches. § Some red dessert wines taste of plum and cherry, making them excellent companions to the darker side of the stone fruit family. These include late harvest or fortified versions of wines like cabernet sauvignon, petite sirah, grenache, black muscat, and zinfandel.

One does a whole painting for one peach and people think just the opposite—that that particular peach is but a detail.

— PABLO PICASSO

selecting fruit

Test fresh stone fruits for flavor by sniffing a ripe sample from the bin if you can't taste one. It should smell sweet and fragrant. Peaches, nectarines, and apricots are just right for cooking when they yield slightly to a gentle push with your finger, though even imperfect or not-quite-soft fruits can be delicious cooked. Steer clear of overripe, mushy, or spongy fruits.

When picked ripe, peaches, nectarines, and apricots show no tinge of green in the background or near the stem. Don't be concerned, though, whether they're predominantly rosy pink or butter yellow. Color and blush indicate variety more than quality. White peaches and nectarines lose their delicate flavor quickly in cooking; they are best enjoyed raw. For neat slices, look for freestone fruits, which release their pits easily, rather than cling varieties.

Cherries are difficult to judge without sampling. Look for firm, shiny fruits with minimal blemishes. Stone fruits are typically at the top of their season during July and August, though cherries begin to appear in spring and some stone fruit varieties are available into fall.

Chilled Stone Fruit Compote

• • •

While you can easily vary this recipe with other fresh, frozen, or dried fruits, this version unmasks the natural sweetness and flavor of stone fruit. Use fruits that are ripe but firm enough to slice without falling apart. If you like, substitute the same wine you will pair with the dessert for some or all of the white grape juice. We love the compote as a sauce over peach or vanilla ice cream.

MAKING THE MATCH

The light stone fruit flavors in the compote lend themselves to a light-bodied wine, such as the delicately sparkling Moscato d'Asti. This would also match well with a fresh late harvest riesling or a lighter ice wine. Stay away from wines that taste strongly of oak or botrytis. Instead, look for a wine that highlights the fruit and summery spirit of this dessert. Hogue Cellars Late Harvest White Riesling (Columbia Valley, Washington) offers a hint of peach and apricot to complement the fruit, along with just a touch of exotic botrytis.

2 medium peaches

2 medium nectarines

2 medium plums

2 medium apricots

½ cup Bing cherries, pitted and halved

¾ cup white grape juice

1 to 4 tablespoons sugar, depending on sweetness of the fruit

Whipped cream, whole-milk yogurt, or crème fraîche

Remove the pits from the peaches, nectarines, plums, and apricots, and cut the fruit into ½-inch-thick wedges. Combine the wedges with the cherries, juice, and 1 tablespoon sugar in a large saucepan. Cook over medium-high heat, stirring occasionally, until the fruit is bubbly and soft but still holds its shape, 10 to 15 minutes. Taste and add sugar as needed, stirring to dissolve. Cool the fruit to room temperature, then cover tightly and refrigerate until cold, at least 2 hours. Serve the chilled compote in stemmed dessert dishes topped with a dollop of whipped cream, whole-milk yogurt, or crème fraîche.

makes 4 servings

Double Plum Galettes

• • •

A galette is a rustic, open-faced tart. Here, almond paste and plum jam complement a mix of red- and yellow-flesh plums. Selecting plums that are ripe but firm, try Santa Rosa or Laroda red plums, and Wickson or Simka yellow ones. Be sure to use jam in the filling; jelly will tend to run out of the tart.

MAKING THE MATCH

Sweet-tart cooked fruit combined with buttery pastry and almond filling are a perfect match with Chambers Rosewood Vineyards Rutherglen Special Muscat (Australia), which has intense plum and prune flavors and a hint of coffee. A black muscat would also be a good choice.

pastry

1 ¼ cups all-purpose flour, plus more for dusting

1 tablespoon wheat germ

½ teaspoon salt

½ cup (1 stick) cold unsalted butter

1 teaspoon pure vanilla extract

¼ cup ice water

filling

3 tablespoons (2 ounces) almond paste (see page 27)

1 tablespoon granulated sugar

½ teaspoon grated lemon zest

2 ½ tablespoons unsalted butter, at room temperature, cut in small pieces

1 large egg

2 tablespoons all-purpose flour

¼ cup plum jam, at room temperature

6 to 8 medium yellow and red plums, skin on, cut into ¼-inch-thick wedges

Powdered sugar or vanilla ice cream

To make the pastry: Combine the 1 ¼ cups flour, wheat germ, and salt in a bowl. Add the butter and use your fingertips to work it into the flour until the butter is in pea-sized pieces. Stir the vanilla into the ice water and drizzle evenly over the flour mixture. Toss with your fingers or a fork, adding a little more water, if needed, to bring the dough together. Toss and press the dough to form a ball, being careful not to overwork it. Turn the dough out onto a lightly floured surface, knead twice, then flatten the dough into a disk and wrap it in plastic film. Refrigerate 20 minutes.

To make the filling: Break up the almond paste with your fingers and place it in the bowl of a standing mixer fitted with a paddle attachment. Add the granulated sugar and lemon zest and mix on medium speed until the almond paste is the texture of coarse sand, about 1 minute. Add half of the butter and mix until smooth, scraping the bowl occasionally. Add the remaining butter. Add the egg and mix until smooth. Mix in the 2 tablespoons flour.

Preheat the oven to 375 degrees F and position two racks in the upper and lower thirds of the oven. Line two baking sheets with parchment paper or silicone baking

mats. Place the chilled pastry on a lightly floured surface and dust the top with flour. Roll the pastry ⅛ to ¼ inch thick and cut out 6 rounds of dough using a saucer or pot lid 5 to 6 inches in diameter as a guide. Gather up the dough scraps and roll again, if needed, to cut the last rounds. Place 3 rounds on each baking sheet.

Use a small offset spatula to smear a thin layer of jam over each pastry round, leaving a ½-inch border. Spread a thin layer of almond filling over the jam. (The jam and almond may blend together.) Arrange alternating layers of red and yellow plums over the filling in a pinwheel fashion. Do not overload them; too much fruit will make the pastry soggy. Fold over ½ inch of pastry around the edges to create a crust, pleating it to fit and covering the filling slightly.

Bake the galettes until the pastry is deep golden brown and crispy on the bottom, 35 to 40 minutes, rotating the pans top to bottom and front to back after about 20 minutes. If the tops threaten to burn, cover the galettes loosely with parchment paper or aluminum foil. Serve the galettes warm or at room temperature, topping each with sifted powdered sugar or a scoop of vanilla ice cream just before serving.

Store the galettes at room temperature, tightly wrapped, for up to 3 days. To crisp them, reheat for 5 to 8 minutes in a pre-heated 350 degrees F oven before serving.

makes 6 servings

Peach Tarte Tatin

• • •

In the patisseries of Paris, we have sampled many a *tarte Tatin* with beautifully caramelized apples showcased atop a flaky, rich crust. We devoted ourselves to creating an easy-to-prepare version as delicious as it is lovely. Here, we apply the winning formula to peaches, which are a natural match with pastry and caramel.

MAKING THE MATCH

This dessert needs a wine with enough body and intensity to stand up to the buttery, flaky pastry and rich caramel, yet enough acidity to cut through all that richness and bring out the fruit's summery spirit. An ice wine fits the bill, and the Joseph Phelps Eisrebe (Napa Valley, California) is a great choice. The wine is made from the scheurebe grape (a cross between sylvaner and riesling) and displays the fruit's floral and peach character. A late harvest white with a touch of botrytis also would match well, such as a Monbazillac or a lighter style Sauternes.

pastry

1¼ cups all-purpose flour

¼ teaspoon salt

½ cup (1 stick) cold unsalted butter, cut into 8 pieces

3 to 4 tablespoons ice water

filling

6 tablespoons (¾ stick) unsalted butter

1 cup sugar

2 large yellow freestone peaches, peeled, halved, and pitted

Ice cream or whipped cream (optional)

To make the pastry: Stir together the flour and salt in a medium bowl. Add the butter and work it with your fingertips into pea-sized pieces, taking care to keep the butter as cold as possible. Slowly drizzle in the ice water, mixing it gently with your fingers in a tossing and lifting motion until a clump of dough will hold together when squeezed. Quickly knead the dough 2 to 3 times, then press into a disk, wrap in plastic film, and refrigerate for at least 15 minutes or up to 3 days.

Preheat the oven to 375 degrees F and position a rack near the center. Arrange four 3-inch tart molds (1 to 1½ inches deep) on a rimmed baking sheet.

To make the filling: In a medium, heavy stainless-steel or anodized aluminum saucepan, melt the 6 tablespoons butter over low heat. (Glazed cast iron retains too much heat and can easily burn the caramel.) Add the sugar, raise the heat a notch, and stir with a flat whisk just to combine. Let the sugar melt undisturbed, stirring only occasionally, as the mixture turns to caramel, 6 to 8 minutes. Continue to cook the caramel a few minutes longer over medium to medium-high heat, stirring

briskly with the whisk and taking care not to splash the butter, until the sugar and butter come together and turn a deep amber color. Remove the caramel from the heat and immediately distribute it among the molds. (It will continue to cook if left in the pot.) Place a peach half, cut-side up, onto the caramel in each mold.

Roll the pastry about ⅛ inch thick on a floured surface using a floured rolling pin. Cut 4 rounds, ½ inch larger than the tops of the molds. (The pastry will shrink as it bakes.) Center one round of pastry over each peach. Bake the tarts on the baking sheet until the crust is deep golden brown and most of the liquid has evaporated, about 50 minutes. Remove the tarts from the oven and immediately invert each onto a serving plate large enough to hold the caramel, which will pool around the pastry. Work carefully, using oven mitts, as the caramel will be scorching hot. Serve warm or at room temperature, topped with ice cream or whipped cream, if desired.

makes 4 servings

Cherry Gêlée Parfait with Lime Custard

• • •

Strawberry nectar and rosé are a natural match in this shimmering gelatin. Cherries give the dessert a contrasting crunch, while lime custard adds creamy richness.

MAKING THE MATCH

Because the gêlée is made with a dry rosé, we like to pair this with something sweet and pink, such as the Palisade Rosé from Plum Creek Cellars (Colorado). Look for a wine with cherry-berry flavors, perhaps with a hint of rose petals. A demi-sec sparkling wine, rosé or not, can offer a lovely textural contrast to the smooth gêlée and rich custard.

cherry gêlée

12 ounces (1½ cups) strawberry nectar (See Note)

2 teaspoons unflavored gelatin

¾ cup dry, light-bodied rosé wine

¼ cup sugar

2 teaspoons finely grated lime zest (about 2 limes)

1 pound Bing cherries, stemmed, pitted, and coarsely chopped

lime custard

2 teaspoons finely grated lime zest (about 2 limes)

1 to 2 tablespoons fresh lime juice

1 cup heavy cream

3 tablespoons sugar

4 large egg yolks, gently whisked

To prepare the cherry gêlée: Pour ½ cup strawberry nectar into a small, wide bowl and sprinkle the gelatin evenly over its surface. Let soften for 5 minutes.

Combine the wine, ¼ cup sugar, 2 teaspoons lime zest, and the remaining 1 cup strawberry nectar in a medium saucepan. Warm over medium heat, stirring occasionally, until the sugar dissolves. Remove the mixture from the heat before it becomes hot. Add the softened gelatin and stir for 1 minute until it is completely dissolved. Pour the gelatin mixture into a medium bowl. Set aside ¼ cup chopped cherries for garnish and stir the remaining cherries into the nectar and gelatin mixture. Cover and refrigerate until softly set, about 6 hours.

To prepare the lime custard: Stir together 1 teaspoon lime zest and a few drops of lime juice to moisten in a small bowl. Cover and set aside for garnish. Heat the cream, 3 tablespoons sugar, and the remaining 1 teaspoon lime zest in a small saucepan over medium heat, stirring occasionally, until the sugar dissolves and the mixture comes to a boil. Remove the pan from the heat.

Quickly whisk ½ cup of the hot cream into the egg yolks until smooth. Pour the cream and egg yolk mixture back into the saucepan and whisk rapidly to avoid scrambling the eggs. Continue whisking over medium heat until the sauce is about as thick as yogurt, about 15 seconds. Remove the custard from the heat and immediately strain it into a small bowl. Place the bowl of custard into a slightly larger bowl filled with ice water. Stir the mixture to cool it, being careful not to slosh water into the custard. Stir in lime juice to taste. Place plastic film directly against the surface of the custard and refrigerate until serving time.

Just before serving, spoon the gêlée and custard into parfait glasses in four alternating layers, ending with the custard. Garnish the parfaits with the reserved chopped cherries and lime zest.

makes 6 servings

Note. You can find strawberry nectar in 12-ounce cans in most supermarkets. When strawberries are in season, consider substituting fresh strawberry purée for the nectar. Blend 2 cups strawberries, ¼ cup sugar (or more to taste), and ⅓ cup water until smooth. Strain and stir in water or rosé wine, if needed, to make 1½ cups.

Buttermilk Panna Cotta with Fresh Peaches

• • •

Panna cotta, or "cooked cream," is quintessentially Italian in its simplicity. The trick is to use just enough gelatin to set the cream without compromising its silky smoothness. Here, buttermilk adds a tangy contrast and peaches complement the wine. You could easily substitute berries, plums, or other fruits in season, varying the wine to match them.

MAKING THE MATCH

Peaches pair well with the muscat canelli grapes used to make Asti and Moscato d'Asti. We love this with La Spinetta Moscato d'Asti (Piedmont, Italy). This also matches well with a delicate late harvest white wine without oak and not too sweet or heavy, such as a demi-sec Vouvray. Look for a wine with fresh stone fruit flavors that pick up on the peaches, rich cream, and tart buttermilk.

Vegetable oil for ramekins

1¼ teaspoons unflavored gelatin (see page 29)

1 cup heavy cream with no additives (see page 28)

¼ cup granulated sugar

1 cup buttermilk

4 ripe yellow peaches, preferably freestone

1 tablespoon light brown sugar

1 teaspoon grated lemon zest

1 tablespoon fresh lemon juice

Lightly oil four 4-ounce ramekins or custard cups. Pour ¼ cup cold water into a small bowl and sprinkle the gelatin evenly over the surface. Let soften for 5 minutes.

Gently warm the cream and granulated sugar in a small, heavy saucepan over low heat, stirring frequently. A drop should feel warm but not hot against your upper lip. Remove the cream from the heat and stir in the softened gelatin for at least 1 minute until it is completely dissolved. Stir in the buttermilk. Divide the mixture among the prepared molds and place them on a plate to cool until they are almost room temperature, about 1 hour. Refrigerate until the panna cotta is set, about 3 hours or up to 4 days. The cream should move in a single jiggle when you shake one of the molds. To avoid condensation, wait until they are completely cold before covering tightly with plastic film.

Prepare the peaches up to 2 hours before serving. Working over a small saucepan to catch their juices, peel the peaches with a sharp knife and cut them into ¼-inch-thick wedges. Gently stir in the brown sugar, lemon zest, and lemon juice a little at a time, adjusting to taste, to bring out the flavor of the peaches. Gently warm the peaches to dissolve the sugar and slightly soften the fruit. Cool to room temperature.

Just before serving, run a thin, sharp knife around the inside of the ramekins to loosen the cream, then invert each into the center of a broad-rimmed soup bowl or serving plate. If the panna cotta does not release easily with gentle tapping, insert the knife between the panna cotta and the ramekin to coax the cream out. Place peach slices decoratively over and around the panna cotta, spooning some of their juices over the top.

makes 4 servings

Jeweled Apricot Soup with Couscous Timbales

• • •

The fruits in this dessert pick up on the exotic floral flavors in many dessert wines, while the earthy couscous is a wonderful complement to botrytis. Look for whole-wheat couscous in health food stores. An assortment of fruits gives the soup a jeweled appearance and a burst of flavor with every bite. Substitute a colorful variety of other fruits in season in similar quantities.

MAKING THE MATCH

We love this dessert with a late harvest botrytised wine that picks up the soup's apricot, exotic fruit, and earthy tones. Freemark Abbey's late harvest riesling, Edelwein Gold (Napa Valley, California), is a great choice, but any late harvest botrytis riesling or Sauternes should pair well. Many ice wines also share these characteristics. Look for rich, long flavors of apricot, tropical fruits, honey, and earth, and for enough body to stand up to this silky soup.

couscous timbales

Vegetable oil for molds

¾ cup plus 2 tablespoons passion fruit nectar

1 tablespoon sugar

½ cup whole-wheat couscous

apricot soup

1¼ cups apricot nectar

⅓ cup fresh orange juice

¼ cup late harvest riesling or other late harvest white wine

1 to 2 tablespoons sugar

1 to 2 teaspoons fresh lemon juice

1½ cups assorted berries (raspberries, blueberries, blackberries, or strawberries)

1 small mango, peeled and cut into ½-inch dice (see page 33)

1 orange, peeled and cut into segments (see page 33)

1 firm-ripe kiwi fruit, peeled and cut into ½-inch dice

To make the timbales: Lightly oil four 4-ounce timbale molds, ramekins, or small coffee cups. Combine the passion fruit nectar and sugar in a small saucepan and bring just to a simmer. Remove from the heat, stir in the couscous, then cover with a tight-fitting lid and set aside for 30 minutes. Fluff the couscous with a fork, then divide it among the molds, packing the grains firmly. Cover the molds with plastic film and refrigerate up to 3 days.

While the couscous is hydrating, make the soup: Stir together the apricot nectar, orange juice, and riesling in a medium bowl. Add sugar and lemon juice to taste.

Set aside 8 of the nicest berries for garnish. Gently stir the mango, orange, kiwi, and the remaining berries into the apricot nectar mixture. Cover and refrigerate until chilled or up to 3 days.

Just before serving, run a thin, sharp knife around the inside of the molds, then invert each timbale into the center of a chilled wide-rimmed soup bowl. Ladle the soup around the timbale in the bowls, distributing the fruit evenly around the couscous. Garnish each timbale with 2 berries.

makes 4 servings

BERRIES

Berries possess a certain immediacy. Picked ripe from the vine during the heat of summer and devoured on the spot, they define instant gratification. With a few additional ingredients and a little ingenuity, they can be transformed into a panoply of desserts, from light and lively to rich and indulgent. § Berries are a varied lot, from cultivated and wild blueberries to fragrant strawberries to sweet-tart raspberries in red or white or sometimes black. Blackberries and their hybrids —boysenberries, marionberries, loganberries, and olallieberries—each have their distinctive charms. § Tart flavors make berries a perfect foil for sweet wines. They tend to match best with lighter wines, yet because most berries are red to purple, they also go well with pink wines and lighter-bodied reds that often show berry flavors. Matched with desserts in this chapter you will find the fizzy pink Brachetto d'Acqui alongside sparklers made from white grapes. Some of the desserts pair well with muscat wines, black and orange muscat, in particular, as well as some of the fortified muscats made in the south of France. A sweet (demi-sec or moelleux) Vouvray often makes a fine pairing. Fortified wines with lower levels of alcohol and lighter botrytised wines match a few of the berry desserts.

You ought to have seen what I saw on my way
                    To the village, through Mortenson's pasture to-day:
Blueberries as big as the end of your thumb,
                    Real sky-blue, and heavy, and ready to drum
In the cavernous pail of the first one to come!

— ROBERT FROST, "BLUEBERRIES"

selecting fruit

The best way to get your hands on sweet, perfectly ripe berries is to pick them yourself or purchase them at a farmers' market. Except for blueberries, berries should be sweet-scented with an aroma characteristic of the varietal. They should look plump and full. While blackberries and kin are often most flavorful when large, blueberries are generally best small. When selecting berries at a market, pick up the basket and inspect it all around to be sure the berries at the bottom are not damaged or moldy. A powdery white coating reveals that blueberries were recently harvested. Because they are fragile, use berries soon after purchasing them.

Boysenberry Sorbet and Cream Swirl

• • •

If fresh boysenberries are not available, substitute blackberries or use frozen, unsweetened boysenberries or blackberries, thawed and drained. If you do not have an ice-cream maker, freeze the sorbet in a 9-by-13-inch glass dish, stirring with a fork every hour until the sorbet is set, about 6 hours. This will produce a granita with an icy texture rather than a smooth sorbet.

MAKING THE MATCH

We like this with a black muscat or a bubbly Brachetto d'Acqui, such as Castello Banfi's Rosa Regale Brachetto d'Acqui (Piedmont, Italy). These wines have good berry flavors and won't be overwhelmed by the cream. In general, avoid very high alcohol wines, which can taste unpleasantly hot with a frozen dessert.

½ cup plus 1 tablespoon sugar

2 tablespoons corn syrup

2 pints (4 cups) fresh boysenberries or blackberries

1 large egg

1 to 3 teaspoons fresh lemon juice

1 cup heavy cream

In a heavy saucepan, combine the ½ cup sugar, corn syrup, and ½ cup water. Bring to a boil over medium heat, stirring occasionally, until the sugar is dissolved, 1 to 2 minutes. Set the syrup aside to cool.

Press the boysenberries through a food mill to purée them and remove most of their seeds. (Alternatively, purée them briefly in a food processor, adding a tablespoon or two of water if needed, and press through a fine-mesh strainer.) Discard the seeds and pulp. Transfer the purée to a container narrow enough so that when you drop in an egg, it will submerge completely.

Stir ¼ cup of the reserved sugar syrup into the berry purée. Using the egg test (see below), add more syrup to the mixture as needed. Remove the egg and stir in lemon juice to taste. Refrigerate the sorbet mixture until it is cold, about 2 hours.

Transfer the sorbet base to an ice-cream maker and freeze according to the manufacturer's directions. If the sorbet is very soft, pack it into an airtight container and place in the freezer until it has the consistency of soft-serve frozen

yogurt. (The sorbet can be stored in the freezer, with wax paper or plastic film pressed against its surface, for up to 2 weeks. Soften at room temperature before proceeding.)

Whip the cream with the remaining 1 tablespoon sugar until it forms soft peaks. Gently fold and swirl the whipped cream into the sorbet using a spatula or spoon. Take care not to mix too vigorously; broad swirls of both sorbet and cream should be visible. Serve immediately.

makes 6 servings

Egg Test for Sorbet. The best sorbets are made not by exact measurements, but rather by balancing the sweetness of a particular batch of fruit to assure the best flavor and consistency. Too much sugar will prevent the sorbet from freezing and will overwhelm the fruit; too little makes an unpleasantly tart, icy sorbet. To achieve the optimal balance, rinse a raw egg and carefully drop it, in its shell, into the fruit mixture. When the mixture is in balance, the egg will be partially floating, exposing a circle the size of a dime to a nickel above the surface.

Raspberry Baked Alaska

. . .

Originally invented as a science experiment demonstrating the insulating power of meringue to prevent a scoop of ice cream from melting when heated, this dessert is said to have received its current moniker from Delmonico's restaurant in New York in honor of the U.S. acquisition of Alaska. Make your own raspberry sorbet (substitute raspberries and omit the cream in the Boysenberry Sorbet recipe on page 53) or use a good quality packaged sorbet.

MAKING THE MATCH

A vintage, or LBV, port with berry flavors is a great complement to the raspberry sorbet. We love this with a young Charles B. Mitchell Vineyards Cucamonga Valley Old Vine Zinfandel Port (California).

Butter and all-purpose flour for coating pan

3 large eggs

6 tablespoons sugar

½ teaspoon pure vanilla extract

¾ cup cake flour, sifted

2 pints raspberry sorbet

5 large egg whites

⅔ cup superfine or granulated sugar

Preheat the oven to 350 degrees F and position a rack in the lower third of the oven. Butter the sides of a 9-inch round cake pan and dust them with flour, tapping out any excess. Line the bottom of the pan with a parchment paper circle and butter the paper. Line a rimmed baking sheet with parchment paper or aluminum foil.

In a standing mixer fitted with the whisk attachment, beat the eggs and 6 tablespoons sugar at high speed until they are thick, pale, and tripled in volume, about 5 minutes. (A handheld mixer may take longer.) Use a whisk to gently but thoroughly fold in the vanilla and flour. Spread the batter evenly in the prepared pan and bake until the cake pulls away from the sides of the pan and the top is golden brown and springs back when pressed lightly near the center, about 20 minutes. Set the pan on a rack until cool, about 20 minutes.

Run a knife around the edges of the cake to loosen it, then invert onto a plate. Remove the parchment paper. With a long serrated knife, cut the cake horizontally into 2 layers using a sawing motion. Place the layers on a flat surface and cut out 8 rounds using a 3-inch cutter. Arrange the rounds on the lined baking sheet. Place a generous scoop of sorbet atop each cake round. Transfer the sheet to the freezer and leave until sorbet is frozen solid, about 1 hour.

Beat the egg whites in an impeccably clean bowl with clean beaters at high speed until they are foamy and just beginning to form soft peaks. Add the ⅔ cup sugar a tablespoon or two at a time, allowing 30 seconds between additions, until it is completely incorporated, scraping the bowl as needed. Continue beating until the meringue is smooth, glossy, and holds stiff peaks.

Remove the cake rounds from the freezer. Working quickly to prevent the sorbet from melting, use a small spatula or knife to completely cover the sorbet and cake, making a good seal with the cake. Swirl the meringue decoratively. Return the baking sheet to the freezer for at least 20 minutes. (The assembled cakes can be frozen in an airtight container for up to 2 weeks.)

Preheat the oven to 500 degrees F and position a rack as low as possible. Transfer the baking sheet to the fully preheated oven and bake until the meringue is well browned, about 5 minutes. Serve immediately.

makes 8 servings

Lemon Raspberry Pavlova

• • •

Legend has it the pavlova was created by a chef in Adelaide, Australia: After watching the Russian ballerina Anna Pavlova, he envisioned a dessert as light and airy as her beautiful movements. Kiwi, passion fruit, and gooseberries are the traditional toppings, but the dessert's snow-white meringue lends itself to endless variations. We've dressed ours up with lemon sorbet and fresh raspberries.

MAKING THE MATCH

This dessert is very delicate even with the whipped cream, which though rich leaves a light impression on the palate. The pavlova is also fairly sweet, so it needs a wine with enough sugar to match or exceed it, and enough acidity to stand up to the lemon and raspberries. We like this with a sweet Vouvray, or a Sauternes or similar wine from that region. Voss Vineyards Botrytis Sauvignon Blanc-Semillon (Napa Valley, California) holds up nicely to both the tart lemon and sweet meringue. A sweet sparkling wine would be another good choice.

Vegetable oil for pan

4 large egg whites, at room temperature

1 cup superfine sugar (see page 29)

2 tablespoons finely grated lemon zest (2 to 3 lemons)

1 tablespoon white vinegar

1 cup heavy cream

2 teaspoons granulated sugar

1 pint lemon sorbet, softened 1 hour in the refrigerator

1 pint (2 cups) fresh raspberries

Preheat the oven to 250 degrees F and position a rack in the lower third of the oven. Line a baking sheet with parchment paper and lightly oil a 10-inch circle in the center of the parchment.

Beat the egg whites in an impeccably clean bowl with clean beaters at high speed until they are foamy and just beginning to form soft peaks. Add the superfine sugar a tablespoon or two at a time, allowing 30 seconds between additions, until it is completely incorporated, scraping the bowl as needed. Continue beating until the meringue is smooth, glossy, and holds stiff peaks, about 15 minutes total. With the mixer at low speed, add the lemon zest and drizzle in the vinegar.

Spoon the meringue onto the oiled area of the parchment and spread into an 8-inch circle. (It will spread as it bakes.) Use the back of the spoon to create a slight indentation in the center and decorative swirls on the surface of the meringue. Bake until the surface is firm and no longer sticky to the touch and sounds hollow when tapped, 65 to 75 minutes.

The meringue should remain snowy white; if it threatens to brown, reduce the temperature to 175 degrees F. When it is done, turn off the oven, leave the oven door closed, and cool completely, 2 hours or up to 1 day.

Use a small baking sheet to carefully transfer the cooled meringue to a platter. (Don't be concerned if a few pieces flake off.) Whip the cream with the granulated sugar to medium-firm peaks. In a large bowl, stir the sorbet to loosen it. Break up any large icy chunks but take care not to melt it; the sorbet should be very thick. Fold in the whipped cream until the mixture is marbled with visible streaks of sorbet and cream. Gently fold in 1 cup of the raspberries.

Fill the center of the shell with the lemon-raspberry swirl and sprinkle the remaining berries over the top. Cut the pavlova into wedges with a sharp serrated knife and use a cake server to carefully transfer the slices to individual plates. Serve immediately.

makes 6 servings

Double Blueberry Crisp Bars

. . .

Perfect for a wine-country picnic, these crisp-chewy bars pack a double blueberry punch from fresh and dried berries. If you can't find dried blueberries that are soft, like raisins, substitute dried cherries or cranberries.

MAKING THE MATCH

A fizzy Brachetto d'Acqui, with its berry flavors, would be a perfect picnic quaff with these bars. Graham's Six Grapes Port (Portugal) is a fine match for the blueberries' jammy qualities.

1 pint (2 cups) fresh blueberries

1 cup dried blueberries

½ cup fresh orange juice (1 to 2 oranges)

¼ cup granulated sugar

2 cups rolled oats

1 cup all-purpose flour

½ cup dark brown sugar, lightly packed

½ teaspoon ground cinnamon

¼ teaspoon salt

½ cup vegetable oil

¼ cup milk

Preheat the oven to 350 degrees F and position a rack near the center. In a medium saucepan, stir together the fresh and dried blueberries, juice, and granulated sugar until the sugar dissolves. Boil, stirring occasionally, until the fresh blueberries give off their juices and the mixture begins to thicken slightly, about 8 minutes. (The filling will thicken considerably as it bakes.) Set aside.

In a medium bowl, stir together the oats, flour, brown sugar, cinnamon, and salt. Add the oil and milk, stirring until the ingredients are evenly moistened. Use your hands (dampened with water, if needed) to press about one-third of the mixture into the bottom of an unbuttered 8-inch square pan in a solid, compact layer. Pour and

spread the blueberry mixture evenly over the bottom crust, then sprinkle the remaining oat mixture evenly over the filling and press it gently into place. Don't worry if some blueberries peek through. Bake until the top is golden brown, 35 to 40 minutes.

Cool the bars at least 30 minutes for easiest cutting. Cut into 5 equal strips in one direction, then 3 in the other, to make 15 bars. Serve warm or at room temperature, or store in an airtight container at room temperature for up to one week.

makes 15 bars

Chilled Strawberry Consommé

• • •

This brilliant, jewel-toned consommé makes a refreshing end to a summer meal. If perfectly ripe berries are not available, use the best frozen berries you can find, preferably individually frozen with no added sugar; thaw them in the bag to retain the juices. This is excellent made a day ahead, as the flavors develop even more with time. Top with strawberry sorbet or a dollop of crème fraîche for extra flavor.

MAKING THE MATCH

This dessert showcases the clean, bright flavor of ripe strawberries. The wine should be similarly light and fresh, with essence of strawberry and other berries. Strawberries and Champagne are a classic pairing, and demi-sec Champagne is a good match here, as is the sparkling Brachetto d'Acqui or a lighter style black muscat. A Muscat de Rivesaltes will pick up on the berries' aromatic floral qualities. We think the rose-colored Inniskillin Cabernet Franc Icewine (Niagara Peninsula, Canada) is a great match.

4 pints (8 cups) fresh strawberries, hulled, or 3 pounds frozen strawberries, thawed

¼ cup sugar

A few drops fresh lemon juice (optional)

4 sprigs fresh mint for garnishing

Slice or dice 2 cups of the berries for garnish; cover and refrigerate. Cut the remaining berries in half.

In a medium nonreactive saucepan, bring the sugar and 3 cups water to a slow simmer over medium-high heat, swirling to dissolve the sugar. Add the halved berries and, if using thawed berries, any juices. Reduce the heat as low as possible, cover, and leave to infuse until the liquid is bright red and the berries have lost most of their color, about 45 minutes. Gently swirl the pot occasionally as they steep, and keep the liquid below a simmer, never boiling, to preserve the fresh berry flavor and avoid clouding the consommé.

Drain the berries through a large, fine-mesh strainer into a nonreactive container to collect the consommé. (Be sure the container does not retain any food odors that could

affect the delicately flavored soup.) Very gently press the berries to extract any remaining juice without pushing any pulp through the strainer. (Discard the spent berries, or save them to serve over ice cream or cereal.) Skim off any foam from the consommé, then taste and stir in a few drops of lemon juice, if needed, to brighten the flavor. Cover and refrigerate until well chilled, about 3 hours. (The consommé can be prepared up to 4 days ahead.)

Scatter the reserved berries among 4 large, shallow soup bowls. Ladle the consommé into the bowls and decorate each with a sprig of mint.

makes 4 servings

Blueberry Almond Tart

• • •

Almond tarts are always popular, and fresh fruit makes them extra dressy and even more wine-friendly. We've started here with a classic almond tart filling and studded it with fresh blueberries, then baked it in a crumbly almond shortbread crust. This is an exceptionally pretty dessert.

MAKING THE MATCH

Look for a wine that marries well with the almond and subtle citrus notes such as an orange muscat or the Domaine de Durban Muscat de Beaumes-de-Venise (Rhône, France). Or play up the blueberry flavors with a sparkling Italian Brachetto d'Acqui or a lighter-style red dessert wine.

almond shortbread crust

¼ cup almonds, toasted and cooled (see page 139)

1 tablespoon granulated sugar

½ cup (1 stick) unsalted butter, at room temperature

⅓ cup powdered sugar plus additional for finishing

1 teaspoon finely grated lemon zest

¼ teaspoon salt

1¼ cups all-purpose flour, plus additional for kneading and rolling

blueberry almond filling

6 tablespoons (about 4 ounces) almond paste (see page 27)

⅓ cup granulated sugar

2 teaspoons finely grated lemon zest

2 teaspoons finely grated orange zest

1 teaspoon pure vanilla extract

½ cup (1 stick) unsalted butter, at room temperature, cut into 6 pieces

2 large eggs

⅓ cup all-purpose flour

¼ teaspoon salt

2 cups blueberries, fresh or frozen (do not thaw)

To make the crust: Grind the almonds and 1 tablespoon granulated sugar in a food processor until very fine. Add the ½ cup butter, ⅓ cup powdered sugar, lemon zest, and salt. Continue processing until the mixture is smooth. Add the 1¼ cups flour and pulse until the dough forms a ball. Turn the dough out onto a floured surface and knead briefly, then wrap in plastic film, press into a disk, and refrigerate until firm, about 40 minutes.

Preheat the oven to 350 degrees F and position a rack in the lower third of the oven. Place a 10-inch fluted tart pan with a removable bottom onto a baking sheet. With a floured rolling pin, roll the chilled pastry into an 11-inch round on a floured board, moving the dough frequently to prevent it from sticking. Use a thin, rimless baking sheet to carefully transfer the pastry to the tart pan. Press the pastry snugly into the pan, pinching together any tears with your fingers. Roll the pin firmly over the top of the pan to neatly trim the edge. Bake until light golden, 15 to 20 minutes. Leaving the oven on, set the crust aside to cool.

While the tart shell bakes, make the almond filling: Break up the almond paste with your fingers. Combine it with the ⅓ cup granulated sugar, lemon zest, orange zest, and

vanilla in a medium bowl. Mix at medium speed until the almond paste is the texture of coarse sand. Add the ½ cup butter one piece at a time, mixing the filling until smooth after each addition and scraping down the bowl as needed. Add the eggs one at a time, mixing until smooth after each one. Mix in the ⅓ cup flour and salt at low speed, then stir in the blueberries by hand

Pour the filling into the tart shell on the baking sheet and bake until the filling is golden brown and the center springs back when lightly touched, about 35 minutes. Transfer the tart to a rack to cool completely.

Remove the outer ring of the tart pan and transfer the cooled tart to a serving platter. Dust with powdered sugar before serving. Cut the tart with a long serrated knife, using a sawing motion. Refrigerate, tightly covered, for up to 1 week; bring to room temperature before serving.

makes 10 servings

CITRUS

In the dead of winter, it's citrus to the rescue! At a time when so many other fruit trees lie dormant, citrus trees blossom and yield their refreshing fruit in abundance. Most citrus fruits are hardy enough to withstand the perils of storage and travel, and reasonably good lemons, limes, oranges, and grapefruit are available year-round. The short season of tangerines makes them the prize of winter, their rinds peeling away easily to reveal segments swollen with bright juice. § Though it may seem like a challenge to pair citrus and wines, these fruits can reinforce the lively acidity that keeps a sweet wine from becoming cloying. Some wines, such as orange muscat, actually taste of citrus. Although the orange in this wine's name refers to the color of the grape, distinguishing it from white and black varieties, it does have the scent of orange blossom and the flavor of citrus. You can depend on it to harmonize with almost any dessert made with orange or that orange would complement. Some late harvest rieslings have lemony flavors that brighten the flavor of desserts. § With lighter citrus desserts, the mildly effervescent Moscato d'Asti is a perfect refreshment, mirroring the dessert without overwhelming it with weight or sweetness. Botrytised wines also pair brilliantly with

A divided orange tastes just as good.

— CHINESE PROVERB

citrus. Honey and lemon are a classic combination, and not just for winter colds. A sip of Sauternes or beerenauslese and a bite of a sweet lemon dessert can evoke a honey-lemon drop, only more exotic and complex.

selecting fruit

Despite the wide availability of storage fruit, citrus is best picked ripe and purchased soon thereafter. Don't be concerned about a tinge of green on the skin; it takes cool nights to set the fruit's bright color. In fact, the tropical or subtropical weather that leaves the fruit green makes it sweeter and less acidic. Sweet, juicy Valencia oranges may actually re-green after ripening. A favorite in California gardens, Meyer lemons are sweeter and more fragrant than the common Eureka or Lisbon lemon. Tangerines range from the nearly seedless and thin-skinned Clementine to the seedy Honey tangerine and the crinkly-skinned Satsuma.

Look for fruit that is heavy for its size, a sign that it will be juicy. Smooth, shiny skins generally mean more fruit and less peel, while fruit that has a thick, pebbly rind is likely to be dry and pulpy inside. Some varieties have wrinkled skin, but they should not feel spongy or light.

Lime Tartlets with Pomegranate Seeds

• • •

Mounded with softly whipped cream and sprinkled with fresh pomegranate seeds, these little tarts are as lovely to look at as they are delightful to eat. Pomegranates appear in markets from October to January. When they are not in season, substitute raspberries.

MAKING THE MATCH

The smooth lime custard and pomegranate seeds are sweet and tart, making a late harvest wine with these same qualities a winning match. The wine should have enough acidity to match the lime and enough weight to stand up to the rich custard and crust. We love these with Wairau River Wines' Marlborough Botrytised Riesling Reserve (New Zealand). The wine is gently honeyed with good body and lively fruit flavors of lime and orange marmalade that perfectly complement the dessert. A not-too-syrupy wine with good acidity and citrus notes from the Sauternes region or an ice wine with similar traits would also be good choices.

cream cheese pastry

½ cup (1 stick) unsalted butter, at room temperature

2 ounces (¼ cup) cream cheese, at room temperature

¼ cup powdered sugar

1½ cups all-purpose flour

¼ teaspoon salt

lime filling

8 large egg yolks

One 14-ounce can sweetened condensed milk

¾ cup fresh lime juice (5 to 6 limes)

1 cup heavy cream

1 tablespoon granulated sugar

1 cup pomegranate seeds (about 1 medium pomegranate) (see page 33)

To make the pastry: Beat the butter, cream cheese, and powdered sugar together in a standing mixer with the paddle attachment until smooth. Add the flour and salt and mix until it comes together into a single mass. (This can also be done in a food processor or by hand.) Turn the dough out onto a flat surface and knead briefly. Divide the dough in half, forming two flat disks. Wrap each disk tightly in plastic film and refrigerate until the dough is chilled and somewhat firm, 45 to 60 minutes.

Preheat the oven to 350 degrees F and position two racks in the upper and lower thirds of the oven. Arrange eight 3-inch tart pans on two rimmed baking sheets. Remove one of the pastry disks from the refrigerator. With a floured rolling pin, roll the dough on a well-floured surface to about ⅛ inch thick. Move the dough frequently as you roll it to prevent it from sticking. With a paring knife, cut four rounds about 1 inch larger than the top of your tart pans.

continued

Lime Tartlets with Pomegranate Seeds (continued)

• • •

You may need to gather up and roll the pastry again to make the fourth round. Use a large spatula or bench scraper to transfer the pastry into the tart pans. Press them firmly into the bottom and sides of the pans, patching any tears with excess dough. Refrigerate the shells while you repeat with the other half of the dough to make a total of 8 tart shells.

Bake the tart shells until they are golden, about 20 minutes, rotating the pans top to bottom and front to back after 10 minutes. Transfer the tart pans to a rack to cool. Reduce the oven to 300 degrees F.

To make the filling: Whisk the egg yolks, sweetened condensed milk, and lime juice in a medium bowl until smooth. Distribute the filling among the tart shells and bake until lightly set, 25 to 30 minutes.

The filling should jiggle slightly when you shake the pan. Place the pans on a rack to cool. Refrigerate the tarts until they are cold, about 2 hours. To avoid condensation, wait until they are completely cold before covering with plastic film.

Just before serving, whip the cream and granulated sugar until the cream holds soft peaks. Remove the tarts from their molds to serving plates. Top each tart with a dollop of cream and a sprinkling of pomegranate seeds. Serve remaining cream and pomegranate seeds in bowls on the side.

makes 8 servings

Hint of Mint Orange Chiffon Cake

• • •

Don't expect the mint in this delightful dessert to jump out at you. Instead, the herb's barely perceptible background note adds complexity to the overall gestalt. It is easiest to zest the oranges before squeezing the juice.

MAKING THE MATCH

Moscato d'Asti perfectly mirrors the delicate, fresh, and fragrant nature of this cake. The Casinetta Vietti Moscato d'Asti (Piedmont, Italy) complements the cake with a floral nose and notes of sweet orange and honeysuckle. An orange muscat also pairs admirably.

1½ cups fresh orange juice (about 3 oranges)

4 sprigs fresh mint, approximately 4 inches long, plus additional mint sprigs for garnishing

Butter and all-purpose flour for coating pan

2 cups cake flour

1½ cups sugar

2 teaspoons baking powder

1 teaspoon salt

8 large eggs, separated

½ cup mild-flavored olive oil

2 tablespoons finely grated orange zest

1 teaspoon pure vanilla extract

1 orange, peeled and cut into thin slices for garnishing

Combine the orange juice and the 4-inch mint sprigs in a wide, shallow nonreactive saucepan. Boil over medium heat until the juice is reduced to ¾ cup, about 15 minutes. Pour the reduced juice into a large mixing bowl and refrigerate until cooled to room temperature. (Alternatively, place the bowl over another bowl filled with ice water to cool the juice more quickly.) Remove and discard the mint.

Preheat the oven to 325 degrees F and position a rack in the lower third of the oven. Butter and flour a 10-inch tube pan, tapping out any excess flour. (Do not neglect this step even if your pan is nonstick, and use butter rather than oil or pan spray.)

Sift together the flour, 1¼ cups of the sugar, the baking powder, and salt. Whisk the egg yolks, olive oil, orange zest, and vanilla into the reduced and chilled orange juice until smooth. Add the dry ingredients and mix until they are well incorporated. Set the batter aside.

In another bowl, beat the egg whites with the remaining ¼ cup sugar at high speed until they form medium peaks that hold their shape but are not quite firm. Stir about one third of the whites into the reserved batter to lighten it, then gently fold in the remaining whites until just a few streaks remain.

Pour the batter evenly into the prepared pan. Bake until a wooden skewer inserted into the center of the cake emerges clean and the top of the cake springs back when pressed lightly, about 50 minutes. The top should be golden brown.

Invert the pan over the neck of a bottle. (Or, if the cake slips out from the pan, transfer it to a rack to cool completely.) Run a knife all around the edges of the pan, including around the center tube. Using your hand to guide it, carefully invert the cake to release it from the pan, and then place it right-side up on a serving platter. Decorate the cake with the additional mint sprigs and orange slices. Use a sharp thin-bladed or serrated knife to cut the cake in a gentle sawing motion.

makes 12 servings

Lemon Thyme Crème Brûlée

• • •

A glassy sugar crust is a dramatic entryway into this smooth, rich custard infused with lemon thyme's intoxicating citrus-herbal essence. Use cream with no additives to help assure that the custard sets properly.

MAKING THE MATCH

This aromatic custard pairs best with a wine having delicate herb and floral notes. It marries beautifully with a Monbazillac or Barsac, or with a Muscat de Beaumes-de-Venise. We love it with the Chateau Lasfons Muscat de Rivesaltes (France). The wine brings out honey and lemon flavors in the dessert, which in turn bring forward delicious bittersweet citrus in the wine.

2 cups heavy cream (see page 28)

½ cup sugar, plus 3 to 4 tablespoons for finishing

½ cup lemon thyme sprigs (about 12 multi-branch stems)

½ teaspoon pure vanilla extract

1 large egg

3 large egg yolks

Preheat the oven to 325 degrees F and position a rack in the lower third of the oven. Fold a tea towel to fit the bottom of a pan that is at least 2 inches deep and large enough to hold 4 wide, shallow crème brûlée dishes or 6-ounce ramekins. Space the ramekins evenly on the towel in the pan.

Combine the cream, ½ cup sugar, and lemon thyme in a small nonreactive saucepan and stir over medium heat until the sugar dissolves and the cream is bubbling around the edges and nearly at a boil. Turn off the heat, cover, and leave to infuse for 15 minutes. Strain the cream into a bowl, discarding the lemon thyme. Stir in the vanilla. Cool to near room temperature, about 30 minutes.

Whisk the whole egg and egg yolks briefly in a medium bowl. Slowly pour the cream into the eggs, whisking constantly, until well blended. Pour the custard through a fine-mesh strainer into a 4-cup glass measure or bowl with a pouring spout. Divide the custard among the ramekins.

Fill a kettle with hot water. Place the baking pan with the ramekins onto the oven rack and carefully pour water into the pan until it reaches about halfway up the ramekins. Drape a single piece of aluminum foil loosely over all the ramekins. Bake until the custards are softly set but jiggle when you shake the pan, 35 to 40 minutes. (Custard in deeper ramekins may take longer.) If some set before others, carefully transfer them to a cooling rack with an oven mitt or sturdy tongs.

Cool the custards on a rack for 30 minutes, then refrigerate until chilled and set, about 2 hours or up to 3 days. To avoid condensation, wait until they are completely cold before covering tightly with plastic film.

Just before serving, sprinkle 2 to 3 teaspoons of the remaining sugar evenly on the surface of each custard. (Wide ramekins will require more sugar than narrow ones.) Holding a propane kitchen torch with the flame about 2 inches from the top of one of the custards, move it slowly and steadily over the surface until the sugar melts and browns, about 2 minutes. Repeat with the others. If you do not have a torch, preheat the broiler, positioning its rack as close as possible to the heating element. Place the ramekins on a rimmed baking sheet and broil the custards, watching and checking frequently, until the sugar melts completely and starts to brown, 2 to 7 minutes. Serve immediately or within 1 hour.

makes 4 servings

Lemon Cream Mousse

• • •

This ethereal mousse is velvet on the tongue. Zingy lemon is the perfect foil to balance the richness of the egg yolks and cream. This recipe works well with either regular lemons or fragrant Meyer lemons. The latter are sweeter; if using them, reduce the sugar by ¼ cup to compensate.

MAKING THE MATCH

Tart lemon and rich dairy call for a wine with a little weight but also enough acid to match the fruit. A late harvest riesling with good acid and lemon undertones pairs well. It is also delicious with a beerenauslese or trockenbeerenauslese, or a Muscat de Rivesaltes. We think it's great with St. Supéry Moscato (Napa Valley, California), made from muscat canelli grapes.

¾ teaspoon unflavored gelatin

¾ cup sugar

¼ cup lemon juice (4 to 6 lemons)

6 large egg yolks

1 cup heavy cream (see page 28)

Pour ¼ cup cold water into a small, wide bowl and sprinkle the gelatin evenly over its surface. Let soften for 5 minutes.

Have on hand a fine-mesh strainer set over a medium bowl. Whisk together the sugar, lemon juice, and egg yolks in the top of a nonreactive double boiler placed over, but not touching, simmering water. Whisk briskly and continuously until the mixture is thick enough that, when you lift the whisk, you see a ribbon rest on the surface before quickly dissolving back into the mixture, about 10 minutes. Strain the mixture and stir in the softened gelatin. Set the warm bowl into a larger bowl half-filled with ice water, making sure not to let water splash into the lemon mixture. Let cool to room temperature, stirring occasionally, about 10 minutes.

Meanwhile, whip the cream to medium peaks. Remove the cooled lemon mixture from the bowl of ice and fold in the whipped cream. Divide the mousse among 6 stemmed glasses or dessert cups. Refrigerate until chilled and set, 1 to 2 hours. The mousse can be refrigerated for up to 3 days. To avoid condensation, wait until it is completely cold before covering with plastic film.

makes 6 servings

Ruby Grapefruit with Honey Sabayon and Lemon Shortbread

. . .

In this light, flavorful dessert, tangy grapefruit is balanced by a honey-sweetened sabayon and buttery lemon shortbread. French sabayon covers a broad family of frothy desserts made with egg yolks and white wine. For the best flavor, use grapefruits that are not especially sour or bitter.

MAKING THE MATCH

This dessert spans a broad range of flavors and textures, from sweet honey to tart citrus, foamy sabayon to crisp shortbread. We enjoy it with King Estate Vin Glacé (Oregon), an ice wine made from pinot gris. The dessert also would work well with an orange muscat or a late harvest riesling with a touch of botrytis and little or no oak.

shortbread

½ cup (1 stick) unsalted butter, at room temperature

¼ cup powdered sugar

1 teaspoon finely grated lemon zest

¼ teaspoon salt

1 cup all-purpose flour

sabayon

2 large eggs

3 large egg yolks

⅓ cup mild-flavored honey

⅓ cup riesling, orange muscat, or other sweet wine

3 medium-large ruby grapefruits, peeled and cut into segments (see page 33)

⅓ cup sliced almonds, toasted and cooled (see page 139)

To make the shortbread: Combine the butter, powdered sugar, lemon zest, and salt in a medium bowl. Using a handheld electric mixer or a standing mixer with the paddle attachment, mix at high speed until smooth, about 30 seconds. Add the flour and continue mixing at medium speed until the dough comes together. (The dough can also be made in a food processor or by hand.) Transfer the dough to a large piece of plastic film. Use the wrap or your floured hands to form the dough into a rectangle approximately 10 inches long, 2 inches wide, and 1 inch thick. Wrap tightly with plastic film and refrigerate until firm, at least 1 hour or up to 1 week.

Preheat the oven to 325 degrees F and position a rack near the center. Line a baking sheet with parchment paper. Unwrap the dough and, with a sharp knife, cut it crosswise into ⅛-inch-thick slices. Arrange the slices evenly on the baking sheet. Bake until the shortbreads just begin to turn light golden brown around the edges, 10 to 12 minutes. Remove to a rack to cool.

To make the sabayon: Whisk together the eggs, egg yolks, honey, and wine in a medium nonreactive metal bowl. Bring about 2 inches of water to a boil in a large saucepan. Fit the bowl snugly in the pan, over but not touching the gently boiling water. Whisk the mixture briskly until it is light, fluffy, and tripled in volume, about 10 minutes. Be sure to move the whisk to the edges of the bowl to keep the entire mixture circulating.

Divide the grapefruit segments among 6 dessert glasses. Spoon the warm sabayon over the fruit and sprinkle with the almond slices. Serve with the shortbread cookies.

makes 6 servings

APPLE & PEAR

"Tastes like biting into a crisp apple." Finally, a wine descriptor we can relate to! Although it can be a stretch to perceive tar, leather, cigar box, horse, or mushroom in wines, biting into an apple and then sipping a wine that tastes of the fruit is a revelation. § Chardonnay is often described as reminiscent of apple, but you might also taste the familiar fruit in riesling, sauvignon blanc, viognier, and other wines, including some sparklers. A wine that tastes of ripe apples is likely to be full-bodied, with plenty of fresh fruit flavor not transformed much by age or oak. A wine that tastes of tart apples, though, is likely to be made from less ripe grapes, their high acidity responsible for the wine's distinctive "green" flavor. Sauvignon blanc works well with the crisp flavors of green apples served fresh or lightly cooked, while some sweet sparkling wines, with their roasted-toasted flavors, bring to mind apple pie. § Where there is apple flavor, pear is often close behind. This combination of flavors helps account for the affinity of many white wines to autumn fruits. The type of wine that will pair best depends on a dessert's other ingredients and method of preparation. Enjoy a dessert of fresh, ripe pears paired with the lightest sweet wines, sparkling or still. Cook those pears and

The golden-rod is yellow,
                    The corn is turning brown,
            The trees in apple orchards
                         With fruit are bending down.

— HELEN HUNT JACKSON, "SEPTEMBER"

the flavors change; a little botrytis might pick up on their mellow sweetness without overwhelming the dessert. If there are nuts, fortified wines might make the best match.

Reminiscent of a cross between an apple and a pear, a quince looks like a hard, fat, knobby pear with a flat bottom. Though not very tasty raw, the fruit's flesh softens and takes on a rosy glow when cooked. It has a musky aroma that pairs beautifully with sweet wines.

selecting fruit

Apples are at their best fresh off the tree during autumn. Pay particular attention to the qualities called for in the recipe: dense or soft flesh, tart or sweet flavor. Dense-fleshed varieties like Granny Smith, Braeburn, and Fuji maintain their shape—important in desserts like the apple terrine—while Jonathan and Macintosh apples cook down to an applesauce consistency. Look for local varieties at farm stands and produce markets. During the summer, New Zealand apples are often a good bet.

Sweet, sensuous pears are one of the few fruits that are best picked and purchased while still hard and green. They ripen best off the tree; tree-ripened pears can be mushy or mealy. When ripe, a pear yields slightly to pressure near its stem. Pears may take a few days to a couple of weeks to ripen on the counter at room temperature. To accelerate the ripening, enclose the pears in a brown paper bag with an apple or banana. Check them frequently, as the window to enjoy them is short: a day or two in the bag can take a pear from perfectly ripe to soft and mealy. Comice and French Butter pears are silky and flavorful; Bosc pears are delightfully crisp when ripe, and maintain their long, elegant shape when poached.

Quince is generally available from late August through November. When ripe, it should be pale yellow but still quite firm. Bigger fruits are often more flavorful.

Individual Pear and Quince Pot Pies

. . .

Sweet pears and fragrant quince are delicious soaked in a wine syrup and sheltered under a flaky golden roof. We love this with buttery smooth but still slightly firm Comice or Bartlett pears. In place of the quince, you can use a tart, dense-fleshed apple or an additional pear; reduce the simmering time to 5 minutes.

MAKING THE MATCH

We make and serve these pies with the same wine to enhance the match. Choose a late harvest riesling with floral notes and without a lot of oak or age, such as the Newlan Vineyards Late Harvest White Riesling (Napa Valley, California). An Alsatian late harvest riesling would also pair nicely.

pastry topping

1 cup all-purpose flour, plus additional flour for rolling

½ cup (1 stick) cold unsalted butter, cut into about 8 chunks

¼ teaspoon salt

2 tablespoons ice water

Butter or oil for ramekins

pear and quince filling

¼ cup late harvest riesling

2½ teaspoons cornstarch

1 quince, peeled, cored, and cut into ½-inch dice

1 cup apple juice

2 tablespoons sugar

2 teaspoons honey

1 teaspoon finely grated lemon zest

2 teaspoons fresh lemon juice

¼ teaspoon salt

2 large pears, peeled, cored, and cut into ½-inch dice

1 tablespoon unsalted butter

About 2 tablespoons milk or cream for glazing pastry

About 2 tablespoons coarse sugar for finishing pastry

To prepare the pastry: Pulse the 1 cup flour, ½ cup butter, and salt in a food processor until the butter is the size of peas. Add the ice water and pulse again, drizzling in up to 2 additional tablespoons of water until the mixture can be pressed into a ball. Transfer the dough to a work surface and knead briefly into a smooth ball, then press it into a flat disk, wrap it in plastic film, and refrigerate until firm, about 30 minutes.

Lightly butter or oil four ramekins or oven-proof dessert dishes that are 3 to 4 inches in diameter and at least 1 inch deep. Place the ramekins on a rimmed baking sheet.

To make the filling: Whisk together the wine and cornstarch in a small bowl; set aside. Combine the quince, apple juice, sugar, honey, lemon zest, lemon juice, and salt in a medium saucepan. Bring to a boil over medium heat, stirring occasionally. Cover, reduce the heat, and simmer until the quince is nearly tender, about 15 minutes.

Add the pears and 1 tablespoon butter, stirring until the butter melts.

Give the cornstarch mixture a quick stir and add it to the fruit filling. Stir for 10 seconds over medium heat, then distribute the filling among the ramekins.

Preheat the oven to 400 degrees F and position a rack in the lower third of the oven. Roll the pastry ¼ inch thick on a lightly floured surface with a floured rolling pin, moving the pastry frequently to prevent it from sticking. (If it is stiff, let it soften for a few minutes.) Cut four pastry rounds to fit the tops of the ramekins.

Place the pastry rounds over the filled ramekins. Brush them lightly with milk and sprinkle them with coarse sugar. Bake until the pastry is deep golden brown, 30 to 35 minutes. Cool about 15 minutes before serving.

makes 4 servings

Apple Citrus Custard Tart

• • •

This exceptionally pretty yet simple tart combines apples with an orange-and-lemon-scented custard in a brown sugar crust. All of the elements combine to bring the flavor of the apples forward. As the tart works well with other seasonal fruit, it serves as a versatile base for exploring other fruit and wine pairings.

MAKING THE MATCH

Tart apple accented by citrus, cream, and brown sugar matches well with a range of wines, from a light, spritzy Moscato d'Asti to an ice wine or a rich late harvest white such as sémillon or sauvignon blanc. We enjoy the tart with the unusual Errazuriz, a late harvest sauvignon blanc from Chile's Casablanca Valley. The nose suggests tropical fruit but the wine has honeyed botrytis with herbal notes that, along with the wine's crisp acidity, make for a lovely match with the tart. An orange muscat would be another good choice.

brown sugar crust

½ cup (1 stick) unsalted butter, at room temperature

½ cup brown sugar, lightly packed

1¼ cups all-purpose flour

½ teaspoon baking powder

½ teaspoon salt

citrus custard filling

1¼ cups heavy cream

¼ cup granulated sugar

1 large egg

3 large egg yolks

1 tablespoon finely grated orange zest

2 teaspoons finely grated lemon zest

1 small (4-inch) vanilla bean, split lengthwise, or ½ teaspoon pure vanilla extract

2 medium-large Granny Smith apples

Powdered sugar for finishing

Preheat the oven to 350 degrees F and position a rack near the center. Place a 9-inch fluted tart pan with a removable bottom on a baking sheet.

To prepare the crust: Cream the butter and brown sugar until smooth, using either an electric mixer or a wooden spoon. Mix in the flour, baking powder, and salt until well blended. Use your hands to press the mixture firmly and evenly into the bottom and sides of the pan. Bake the crust until golden brown, about 20 minutes. Leaving the oven on, set the crust aside.

To make the custard: Whisk together the cream, sugar, whole egg, egg yolks, orange zest, and lemon zest in a medium bowl. Scrape in the seeds from the vanilla bean with a sharp paring knife (reserve the pod for another use), or add the vanilla extract. Stir to combine.

Working around the core and leaving it behind, cut each apple in four large pieces; do not peel them. Cut the pieces lengthwise into very thin slices. Fan the slices and arrange them in the baked tart shell to completely cover the bottom.

Place the tart on the baking sheet in the oven and slowly pour the custard over the apples to fill the shell. (Bake any excess custard separately.) Carefully close the oven, reduce the temperature to 300 degrees F, and bake just until the custard is set, about 55 minutes. To test, press your finger lightly near the center; the filling should not feel liquid.

Transfer the pan to a rack to cool the tart completely. Cover and refrigerate until chilled, about 2 hours. Remove the outer rim of the tart pan and dust the tart with powdered sugar just before serving.

makes 8 servings

Baked Granny Smith Apple Terrine

• • •

We dressed up the classic baked apple, baking the fruit in a terrine for a more formal presentation of this perennial favorite. Buttered pecans add crunch and a hint of salt that brings the flavors together. We love this with thick Devonshire cream (available in specialty food stores), crème fraîche, or a scoop of vanilla or cinnamon ice cream. If you substitute another apple for the Granny Smiths, be sure to use a variety that is similarly dense and tart.

MAKING THE MATCH

A vin santo such as the Brolio Vin Santo del Chianti Classico (Tuscany, Italy) is a great match for this combination of sweet-tart apple, caramel, and buttery toasted pecans. A tawny port or Madeira also brings out the roasted nut and praline flavors. Many late harvest white wines sport apple flavors, making them another fine match. Consider a fresh or lightly botrytised late harvest riesling from Alsace or Germany, or a muscat.

¼ cup (½ stick) plus 1 tablespoon unsalted butter

1 cup sugar

5 to 6 medium (about 2½ pounds) Granny Smith apples, peeled, cored, and cut in 2½-inch-thick slices

½ cup coarsely chopped pecans

⅛ teaspoon salt

Preheat the oven to 375 degrees F. Have ready an 8½-by-4½-by-2½-inch ungreased loaf pan by the stove. (Avoid aluminum pans, which can impart a metallic taste.)

Melt the ¼ cup butter in a large, heavy saucepan over medium heat. (Avoid glazed cast iron, as it retains too much heat and can easily burn the caramel.) Add the sugar and let it melt, stirring only occasionally as the mixture turns to caramel, about 10 minutes. Continue cooking, stirring briskly with a whisk, until the sugar and butter come together and turn a deep caramel color, 5 to 10 minutes longer. Take care not to slosh the butter or burn the caramel; it will continue to cook after you remove it from the heat. Immediately pour the hot caramel into the loaf pan. (Be cautious; the caramel will be extremely hot.)

Make a neat layer of apples on top of the caramel—the bottom will be the top when you serve it—then pack the remaining apples tightly into the pan, mounding them over the top. Cover the pan with aluminum foil, cutting several slits in the foil to let steam escape. Place the pan on a baking sheet to catch any bubbling caramel and bake for 30 minutes. Remove the foil and continue baking until the apples are soft and most of the moisture has evaporated, about 45 minutes longer.

While the terrine bakes, melt the 1 tablespoon butter in a small cast-iron or heavy ovenproof skillet. Add the pecans and salt, tossing to coat the nuts evenly. Place the pan in the oven alongside the terrine until the cut edges of the nuts are golden, 6 to 10 minutes. Transfer the pecans to a plate lined with a paper towel to cool.

Transfer the terrine to a rack and let cool in the pan for 45 to 60 minutes. Cover it with plastic film, pressing it directly against the surface, and place on a plate to catch any spills. If you have a second loaf pan that will fit snugly on top of the terrine, place it in the pan and use cans from your pantry to weight it. Otherwise, place the weights directly on the plastic film as evenly as possible. Refrigerate overnight.

To serve, place the chilled loaf pan on the stove over medium heat for 5 seconds to loosen the caramel. Run a knife around the sides of the pan, then invert the terrine onto a serving platter with a raised edge to catch any caramel. Give the pan a tap to release the terrine. Use a long serrated knife to slice the terrine. Sprinkle the slices with buttered pecans.

makes 6 servings

Deconstructed Autumn Pear Crisp with Sparkling Pear Sorbet

• • •

This light, refreshing dessert combining uncooked pears with a crisp topping is perfect for a warm autumn evening. On cold winter nights, gently warm the pears in the microwave or oven before composing the dessert. Use a sparkling pear or apple cider with good fruit flavor and no added sugar. If you do not have an ice-cream maker, use the mixture to prepare a granita.

MAKING THE MATCH

Ripe pears, hints of lemon, a crisp cinnamon topping, and icy sorbet make a Moscato d'Asti, such as Michele Chiarlo's delightful Nivole (Piedmont, Italy), a winning match. The wine's low alcohol and slight fizz bring out the fresh flavors of the dessert. A late harvest riesling with no oak or botrytis would be another good match.

pear cider sorbet

¼ cup granulated sugar

2 cups sparkling pear cider

2 teaspoons fresh lemon juice

topping

¾ cup all-purpose flour

½ cup rolled oats

⅓ cup light brown sugar, lightly packed

1 teaspoon ground cinnamon

¼ teaspoon salt

6 tablespoons (¾ stick) unsalted butter, at room temperature, cut into large pieces

4 large red pears, ripe but still firm

1 to 2 teaspoons fresh lemon juice

Powdered sugar for finishing (optional)

To prepare the sorbet: In a nonreactive saucepan, heat the granulated sugar and ¼ cup water together over medium-high heat, stirring until the sugar is completely dissolved. Stir in the cider and lemon juice. Cover and refrigerate until cold, then freeze in an ice-cream maker according to the manufacturer's directions.

Preheat the oven to 325 degrees F and position a rack near the center. Line a baking sheet with parchment paper.

To make the topping: Mix together the flour, oats, brown sugar, cinnamon, and salt in a medium bowl. Add the butter and rub the mixture with your fingertips until the butter is well distributed throughout. Gather the mixture into a single mass as if for pie pastry, then crumble it between your fingers until it has the texture of granola. Spread the mixture on the baking sheet and bake until the crumble is light golden brown, 25 to 30 minutes. Let cool completely, breaking up any large chunks with your fingers. Set aside.

Just before serving, halve the pears. Use a melon baller to remove the cores and stems. Lay the pear halves cut-side down on a cutting board and cut lengthwise into paper-thin slices. (Use a mandoline if you have one.) Put the pear slices in a bowl and sprinkle them with 1 teaspoon lemon juice. Toss very gently, adding a little more lemon juice if needed to lightly coat them.

Pile the pear slices in an attractive arrangement in eight wide, shallow dessert bowls. Top the pears generously with the crumble topping. If desired, sift powdered sugar over them. Use two tablespoons to form egg-shaped scoops of sorbet, and place a scoop or two on each plate. (If you made a granita, you may need to use an ice-cream scoop.) Serve immediately.

makes 8 servings

Ginger Pears with Black Sesame Butter Crunch

• • •

Use full-flavored pears, such as Comice, French Butter, or Bartlett, to balance the zesty ginger in the compote. The pears should yield to light pressure but not be too soft. Look for black sesame seeds in Asian markets or health food stores. They have great flavor and make a dramatic looking wafer, but brown or white sesame seeds will work equally well.

MAKING THE MATCH

This is a good dessert for a lighter style wine that echoes toasted sesame, butter, or pear flavors. A late harvest riesling is a good choice, as is a sweet Vouvray, a sweet sparkling wine, or a cream sherry to bring out the nutty sesame in the butter crunch. Veuve-Clicquot Ponsardin Champagne Demi-Sec (France) pairs well.

black sesame butter crunch

½ cup all-purpose flour

2 tablespoons cornstarch

¼ teaspoon salt

⅓ cup black sesame seeds

¼ cup (½ stick) unsalted butter, at room temperature

⅔ cup dark brown sugar, lightly packed

ginger pears

4 medium pears, peeled, cored, and cut into ½-inch dice

¼ cup late harvest riesling wine

2 to 4 tablespoons granulated sugar

¾ teaspoon dried ground ginger

1 teaspoon finely grated lemon zest

2 to 3 teaspoons fresh lemon juice

1 small (4-inch) vanilla bean, split lengthwise (optional)

To make the butter crunch: Preheat the oven to 325 degrees F and position a rack near the center. Line a 17-by-12-inch baking sheet with a silicone baking mat or parchment paper. Sift together the flour, cornstarch, and salt. Stir in the sesame seeds and set aside.

Cream the butter and brown sugar until smooth. Add 2 tablespoons water and the flour–sesame seed mixture; blend just until incorporated.

Spread the batter evenly on the prepared baking sheet with a palette knife or spatula to make a single slab that is ⅛ to ¼ inch thick, taking care not to thin the wafer toward the edges. Bake until deep golden brown all over, about 20 minutes. Immediately invert the baking sheet onto paper towels on a flat surface. Wait about 30 seconds, then carefully peel away the silicone mat and cool the

wafer until crisp, about 15 minutes. Break the wafer into 12 odd-shaped pieces.

To make the ginger pears: Place the pears, wine, 2 table-spoons of the granulated sugar, ginger, lemon zest, and 2 teaspoons of the lemon juice in a medium nonreactive saucepan. Use a knife to scrape the seeds from the vanilla bean (if using) into the pot. (Reserve the pod for another use.) Bring the mixture to a boil over medium-high heat, then reduce the heat to low and simmer, stirring occasionally, until the pears are tender but still retain their shape, 5 to 7 minutes. Taste the compote and add sugar or lemon juice, if needed.

Serve warm, or cover and refrigerate until chilled, 1 to 2 hours. Serve the compote in dessert bowls with the butter crunch wafers on the side.

makes 6 servings

TROPICAL FRUITS

While tropical fruits may seem exotic and mysterious, they are anything but strangers to wine. Many dessert wines, in particular, have rich flavors of pineapple, lychee, mango, kiwi, coconut, or other tropical fruits. § Tropical fruits contribute background flavors to many chardonnays and dry wines made from other grapes. In dessert wines, aromatic sweetness and more developed flavor bring the fruits' exotic essence into clear focus. Riesling and vidal grapes contribute a tropical perfume to ice wines. Quarts de Chaume and other chenin-blanc-based Loire wines, gewürztraminers, and botrytised wines can sport tropical fruit flavors. § Wines with a tropical fruit profile tend to marry well with other fruits in the family. Don't hesitate to pair a wine featuring flavors of pineapple or lychee with a mango dessert, for example. Wines tasting of other perfumed fruits, especially apricot, also pair well. Fragrant wines like malvasia bianca, muscat, sémillon, and viognier are delicious with these desserts.

Bees don't swarm in a mango grove for nothing.

Where can you see a wisp of smoke

without a fire?

— HLA STAVHANA, "THE GTHSAPTAAT OF STAVHANA HLA"
(translated by Martha Ann Selby)

selecting fruit

The skin of a ripe mango, depending on the variety, can range in color from green with a red blush to solid yellow. The best way to detect a mango's flavor and ripeness is to sniff near the stem for the fruit's distinctive fragrance. A ripe mango will yield to light pressure but should not be completely soft. For slicing, use fragrant fruits that are still somewhat firm. An unripe mango will generally ripen on the counter within a week. To accelerate ripening, place the fruit in a paper bag with a banana or apple. See page 33 for advice on cutting a mango.

Pineapples also can be selected by their fragrance at the stem end. Look for fruit that has fresh, green leaves and is free of soft spots and bruises. When ripe, a pineapple will give slightly when pressed. If the fruit smells as if it is beginning to ferment, it is overripe. The peeled and cored pineapples often available in plastic containers in supermarket produce sections can be a great time-saver.

Mango-Lime Soufflés

• • •

Magical meringue makes these miniature soufflés come to life in the oven. Made with an all-fruit base (no yolks or cream), they are ideal for those on a restricted fat diet. But make no mistake—these soufflés are luxuriously satisfying. These can be dressed up with a sauce made by mixing additional mango purée with a little sugar and lime juice. Poke a hole in the top of the finished soufflé and pour in the sauce just before serving.

MAKING THE MATCH

Choose a light-bodied wine that will not overwhelm the dessert, such as a malvasia bianca or a demi-sec Champagne. A lighter style ice wine with tropical fruit flavors would also be a good match. We enjoy this with Bonny Doon Vineyard's icebox wine (faux ice wine), Vin de Glacière (Santa Cruz, California).

Butter and granulated sugar for coating molds

2 tablespoons cornstarch

3 ripe mangoes, peeled

6 tablespoons granulated sugar

2 teaspoons finely grated lime zest (about 2 limes)

2 tablespoons fresh lime juice

4 large egg whites

Powdered sugar for finishing

Preheat the oven to 400 degrees F and position a rack to leave plenty of room above it for the soufflés to rise. Lightly butter and sugar eight 6-ounce ramekins, tapping out excess sugar. Place the ramekins on a rimmed baking sheet.

In a small bowl, whisk the cornstarch into 3 tablespoons cold water until smooth and set aside. Cut 1 mango into ¼-inch cubes and set aside (see page 33). Coarsely chop the flesh from the remaining 2 mangoes and purée in a blender until smooth (a food processor will not break down the fibers as well) to make about 1 cup of mango purée.

Bring the mango purée and 3 tablespoons of the sugar to a boil in a nonreactive saucepan over medium heat. Give the cornstarch-water mixture a quick stir, then whisk it into the purée. Stir and cook until the mixture comes back to a boil, then cook 1 minute longer until thickened. Remove from the heat and stir in the lime zest, lime juice, and the reserved mango cubes. Set aside.

Whip the egg whites with the remaining 3 tablespoons sugar at high speed until they form medium peaks that hold their shape but are not quite stiff. Working gently and quickly to avoid deflating the whites, fold one-third of the whites into the mango purée, then fold the purée back into the whites until only a few streaks of egg white remain.

Spoon the soufflé mixture evenly into the prepared ramekins. Fill the ramekins to the top, then sweep the back of a knife across the top to smooth and level them. Run your thumb around the inside edge of each ramekin to form a slight indentation around the inside rim.

Bake the soufflés on the baking sheet until they are just set in the center and golden on top, 12 to 15 minutes. To test for doneness, use a paring knife to pry up the top of a soufflé and look inside; it should appear softly set. Dust the hot soufflés with powdered sugar and serve immediately.

makes 8 servings

Fresh Mango-Nectarine Crumble

• • •

In this twist on the typical crumble, we've baked up a buttery topping to be scattered atop macerated fruit just before serving. Try adapting this with other fruits in season—peaches and blackberries, apricots and cherries, mango and crushed lychees, Fuyu persimmons and seedless tangerines.

MAKING THE MATCH

The fresh fruit and buttery topping pair well with many wines, from a light muscat to a rich ice wine. Audubon Cellars Late Harvest Chardonnay (California) mirrors both the tropical and stone fruit flavors in this dessert.

crumble topping

1 cup all-purpose flour

⅓ cup sugar

¼ teaspoon salt

½ cup (1 stick) unsalted butter, at room temperature, cut into 8 pieces

½ teaspoon pure vanilla extract

fruit

2 ripe mangoes, peeled and cut into julienne strips (see page 33)

2 ripe nectarines, cut into paper-thin slices

¾ cup Moscato d'Asti, or the wine you will serve with the dessert

¼ to ½ cup sugar

1 teaspoon finely grated lime zest

2 teaspoons fresh lime juice

To make the crumble topping: Preheat the oven to 350 degrees F. Stir together the flour, sugar, and salt in a medium bowl. Add the butter and sprinkle evenly with the vanilla. Use your fingertips to pinch and rub the butter into the flour until the mixture looks like coarse cookie crumbs. Spread the crumble onto an ungreased baking sheet, squeezing a bit to make granola-like clumps. Bake until golden brown, 15 to 20 minutes, stirring once or twice for even baking. Place the baking sheet on a rack to cool.

While the topping bakes, prepare the fruit: Combine the mango and nectarine pieces in a medium bowl. Add the wine, ¼ cup sugar, lime zest, and lime juice, and stir gently to avoid breaking up the fruit, adding sugar to taste, if needed.

Pile the fruit into six dessert cups and drizzle each with a tablespoon or two of the juices from the bowl. Scatter the crumble topping over the fruit.

makes 6 servings

Tropical Fruit Crêpes

. . .

Tender crêpes filled with a tropical fruit ambrosia makes a wonderfully elegant yet simple dessert. A classic crêpe is not permitted to brown; however, a little color on the first side makes for a pretty presentation, adds flavor, and firms the crêpe for easier turning. Cut the fruit evenly into ¼-inch dice for a pretty filling of bite-sized fruit.

MAKING THE MATCH

Select a late harvest white wine or an ice wine with enough body to match the cream and sufficient acidity to accent the fruit filling. Although late harvest chardonnays are hard to come by, the grape often develops tropical fruit flavors, as do rieslings from the Pacific Northwest. We love this with Beringer Nightingale (Napa Valley, California), a sémillon-sauvignon blanc blend sprayed with botrytis to create a Sauternes-style wine.

crêpe batter

½ cup all-purpose flour

1 teaspoon granulated sugar

Pinch of salt

1 extra-large egg

About ⅔ cup whole milk

1 tablespoon vegetable oil, plus additional oil for the pan

filling

¼ cup sweetened shredded coconut

¾ cup diced fresh papaya

¾ cup diced fresh mango

¾ cup diced fresh pineapple

¾ cup diced fresh kiwi fruit

¼ cup granulated sugar

2 tablespoons pineapple juice or 1 tablespoon fresh lime juice

½ cup heavy cream, whipped to medium-stiff peaks

Powdered sugar for finishing (optional)

Toasted, sliced almonds for garnishing (optional)

To make the crêpes: Whisk together the flour, granulated sugar, and salt in a medium bowl. Whisk in the egg and 1 or 2 tablespoons of the milk to form a smooth paste. Whisk in the remaining milk and the 1 tablespoon vegetable oil. The batter should have the consistency of heavy cream. If it is too thick to produce thin crêpes, or thickens as you work, stir in more milk, a tablespoon or two at a time.

With a brush or folded paper towel, coat a 6-inch nonstick pan with a thin layer of oil. Place the pan over medium heat until it is hot, about 1 minute. Lift the pan away from the heat and swirl it as you ladle in about ¼ cup batter, just enough to coat the bottom of the pan in a thin layer. (Pour excess batter back into the bowl.) Return the pan to

the heat and cook until the crêpe slides easily in the pan and begins to color, 1 to 2 minutes. Use a heat-resistant spatula to loosen the edges or to slide under the crêpe if it sticks.

Turn the crêpe over and heat just until it is cooked through, about 30 seconds. (Do not be concerned if your first crêpe is not perfect. Even for professional chefs, the first is almost always a throwaway. As the pan heats and develops its oiled surface, the crêpes should release more easily.) Invert the crêpe onto a large plate. Between crêpes, wipe the pan with a paper towel to remove any remaining bits of crêpe and add a little more oil, brushing or wiping to coat the pan. Continue making and stacking the crêpes until all the batter is used. You should have

continued

Tropical Fruit Crêpes (continued)

• • •

about 12 crêpes. (Once cooled, they can be wrapped in plastic film and refrigerated for up to 2 days. Warm them, one at a time, in a slightly oiled skillet.)

To prepare the filling: Toast the coconut in a small skillet over medium-low heat, shaking and stirring frequently, until it is lightly browned. Transfer to a medium bowl. Add the papaya, mango, pineapple, and kiwi fruit. Stir the granulated sugar into the pineapple juice, then pour the juice over the fruit mixture and toss to coat evenly. Fold the whipped cream into the fruit and refrigerate for up to 4 hours. (Alternatively, keep the cream and fruit separate and layer the fruit over the cream inside the crêpes to serve.)

To serve, place a crêpe, prettiest-side down, on a dinner plate. Spread ¼ cup of the fruit filling in a strip down the center of the crêpe. Fold the two sides over the filling to overlap, then carefully transfer the crêpe to an individual serving plate. Repeat with remaining crêpes and filling. Dust with powdered sugar and sprinkle with almonds, if using. Serve immediately.

makes 6 servings

Ginger Pots de Crème

• • •

Pot de crème refers to the little covered porcelain pot that traditionally contains this rich custard. Custards provide a perfect background for highlighting clean, bright flavors. For this one, we infuse ginger into cream for a spicy twist. Because ginger has a tendency to curdle cream, avoid heating the milk after adding it.

MAKING THE MATCH

This dessert pairs best with a wine that can stand up to its richness and spice. A trockenbeerenauslese, Sauternes, or Hungarian Tokaji works well. Royal Wine Company Tokaji Aszú 5 Puttonyos (Hungary) complements the dessert well, while a demi-sec Champagne is a great way to refresh the palate.

2 cups heavy cream (see page 28)

½ cup sugar

2 tablespoons coarsely grated fresh ginger

1 large egg

4 large egg yolks

Pinch of salt

Preheat the oven to 300 degrees F and position a rack in the lower third of the oven. Fold a tea towel to fit the bottom of a pan that is at least 2 inches deep and large enough to hold six 4-ounce pot de crème pots, oven-proof espresso cups, or ramekins. Space the six cups evenly on the towel in the pan.

Heat the cream and sugar in a small nonreactive saucepan just until the mixture is very hot, with small bubbles forming around the perimeter. Remove from the heat, stir in the ginger, cover, and leave to steep for 15 minutes.

Whisk together the whole egg, egg yolks, and salt in a small bowl, then pour them in a slow stream into the cream as you whisk constantly. Pour the mixture through a fine-mesh strainer into a 4-cup glass measure or bowl with a pouring spout, pressing on the ginger to extract its flavor.

Pour the custard into the pots or ramekins. Fill a kettle with hot water. Place the pan with the custards onto the oven rack and pour in hot water to reach about a third of the way up the sides of the pots. Cover the pots with their lids or place a piece of aluminum foil loosely over the custards. Bake until the custards are set around the edges but jiggle in the middle when you shake them, 30 to 40 minutes. If some are done before others, use an oven mitt or sturdy tongs to carefully transfer them to a cooling rack. Cool the custards for 30 minutes, then refrigerate until they are set and chilled through, about 90 minutes longer or up to 4 days. To avoid condensation, wait until they are completely cold before covering tightly with plastic film.

makes 6 servings

Brown Sugar Glazed Bananas with Roasted Peanuts and Lime

• • •

This exceedingly quick and easy recipe blends sweet, sour, and salty flavors. It is a great way to use up bananas before they get too ripe. We like to make this with the small finger bananas, sometimes called niño or baby bananas, and top them with a scoop of coconut or white chocolate ice cream. Avoid roasted peanuts that contain seasonings such as paprika or garlic salt.

MAKING THE MATCH

Sweet wines love salt, and the bananas pair well with botrytis. Together, the elements match well with a late harvest botrytised wine with good acidity, such as a sauvignon blanc or sémillon. We love this with Carmenet's honey-gold Copa de Oro late harvest sémillon (Edna Valley, California). The combination of flavors also stands up well to a vin santo or tawny port, while the lime marries nicely with orange muscat or a late harvest white featuring citrus flavors.

4 medium bananas or 8 niño bananas, completely yellow with just a few dark spots

½ cup light brown sugar, lightly packed

⅓ cup salted, dry roasted peanuts, coarsely chopped

2 teaspoons finely grated lime zest (about 2 limes)

¼ cup (½ stick) unsalted butter, cut into small pieces

2 to 3 tablespoons fresh lime juice

Preheat the broiler and position an oven rack 6 to 8 inches from the broiler element. Butter a rimmed baking sheet or line it with foil.

Peel the bananas. Cut them in half crosswise and then lengthwise to make four pieces for each banana. (If using niño bananas, cut them in half lengthwise only.) Place the bananas cut-side up in the prepared pan. Sprinkle the brown sugar, peanuts, and lime zest evenly over the bananas. Dot them with the butter pieces and drizzle with 2 tablespoons of the lime juice.

Broil the bananas until the sauce is bubbling and patches of brown appear on the peanuts and bananas, 3 to 5 minutes. Sprinkle the bananas with the remaining lime juice and serve immediately on warm plates.

makes 4 servings

Coconut-Lychee Tapioca Pudding

• • •

Juicy-sweet lychees are a great foil to this rich (yet dairy-free) pudding. The recipe calls for chilling the pudding, which will thicken it, but don't hesitate to indulge while it's warm. This recipe uses small pearl tapioca, about ⅛ inch in diameter. If you use a large pearl variety, plan on about 15 minutes additional cooking time. Instant or quick-cooking tapioca and lite coconut milk do not work in this recipe.

MAKING THE MATCH

Many late harvest white wines remind us of tropical fruits, lychee in particular. The tropical fruit flavors in Stony Ridge Malvasia Bianca (Livermore Valley, California) makes it a delicious match. It would also be delightful with an ice wine, but to ensure the match isn't cloying, choose one with enough acid to complement the richness of the coconut milk and bring out the lychee flavor rather than drowning it.

½ cup small pearl tapioca

One 20-ounce can whole lychees in heavy syrup

One 14-ounce can unsweetened coconut milk (about 1¾ cups)

¼ cup sugar

½ teaspoon salt

½ teaspoon pure vanilla extract

Mint sprigs for garnishing (optional)

Stir together the tapioca and 3 cups of room temperature water in a medium bowl. Leave to soak for 30 minutes. (A shorter soaking may result in a pudding that is too sticky; longer and it may be too thin.) Pour the pearls into a strainer and rinse under cool running water. Set aside.

Pour off ¾ cup syrup from the lychees and set aside. (Save the rest for another use.) Set aside 6 whole lychees for garnish, then tear the rest into pieces, 4 to 6 per fruit. Shake the can of coconut milk vigorously, then pour off ½ cup. Cover and refrigerate the 6 whole lychees and ½ cup coconut milk.

Pour the reserved ¾ cup lychee liquid, the remaining coconut milk, and 1¼ cups cool water into a large, heavy saucepan. Stir in the sugar, salt, and lychee pieces with a wooden spoon. Bring to a slow simmer over medium heat. Add the drained tapioca pearls, stirring occasionally to prevent them from sticking to the bottom of the pot.

When the mixture almost returns to a simmer (avoid boiling it once the tapioca is added), reduce the heat and cook just below a simmer, stirring occasionally, until the tapioca pearls are translucent and tender to the bite, about 10 minutes longer. The pudding will have a loose consistency; it will thicken as it chills.

Stir in the vanilla, then pour the pudding into a wide, shallow bowl and refrigerate until chilled and set, at least 6 hours or overnight. (The pudding can be refrigerated in an airtight container for up to 2 days.)

Just before serving, whisk the reserved ½ cup coconut milk to break up any lumps, then gently fold it into the pudding. Scoop the pudding into individual dessert dishes and top each with one of the reserved lychees and a sprig of mint, if desired.

makes 6 servings

DRIED FRUITS

Left late on the vine, grapes embark on a slow transformation into raisins. Not all grapes intended for sweet wines dry completely, but in the process of ripening most begin to dehydrate, concentrating their flavors into the lush nectars we enjoy at the end of a meal. § Whether the concentration of flavor comes from drying the grapes on mats, withering from botrytis, freezing out the water, or simply by hanging on the vine long enough to develop an intense sweetness, it should come as no surprise that wines made from these grapes taste of dried fruit. Dessert wines may have flavors of dried apricot, plum, cherry, berry, fig, or, of course, raisin. Grapes dried while on the vine, spread on racks or mats, or hung in cellars give vin santo, Italian *passito* wines, and French *vins de paille* their distinctive flavors. Many fortified wines also have an affinity for dried fruits by virtue of their nutty and concentrated fruit flavors.

Life's a pudding full of plums;

Care's a canker that benumbs,

Wherefore waste our elocution

On impossible solution?

Life's a pleasant institution,

Let us take it as it comes!

— SIR WILLIAM SCHWENCK GILBERT, "THE TANGLED SKEIN"

selecting dried fruit

The dried fruit most of us know best from childhood is the raisin. These days, store shelves are stocked not only with the more familiar apricots, dates, figs, and plums (or prunes), but with all manner of exotic dried fruits: mangoes, papayas, pineapples, nectarines, currants, cranberries, and cherries both sweet and tart.

Select fruits that are moist and pliable. Many dried fruits are treated with sulfur compounds to preserve their color and moist texture. While sulfured fruits often resonate with wines—which have similar flavors from natural sulfites and sulfurs used in the winemaking process—we choose untreated fruits for their truer flavor. Prechopped fruits tend to sacrifice flavor for convenience.

Holiday Dried and Fresh Fruit Tartlets

· · ·

As these fruit-filled tartlets bake, their wafting aroma will convince you that you have perfectly captured the spirit of the holidays in your kitchen. But unlike that other holiday staple, passed in perpetuity among friends, these will quickly disappear behind satisfied smiles.

MAKING THE MATCH

The brandy in these tarts makes them a good match with fortified wines. We love them with vin santo, a sweet sherry, or a tawny port, such as Warre's Otima 10 Year Old Tawny Porto (Portugal). Be sure the wine has enough body to match the richness of the dried fruit.

pastry crust

6 tablespoons (¾ stick) unsalted butter, at room temperature

¼ cup powdered sugar

¼ teaspoon ground cinnamon

¼ teaspoon salt

1 large egg

1 cup all-purpose flour

fruit filling

1 small red apple, such as Braeburn, Fuji, or Rome, diced, with peel

1 small red pear, such as Red Sensation or Red Bartlett, diced, with peel

⅓ cup dried figs, coarsely chopped

⅓ cup dried apricots, coarsely chopped

¼ cup currants

¼ cup dried cranberries or cherries

1 small (4-inch) vanilla bean, split lengthwise

⅓ cup granulated sugar

⅓ cup brandy

1 teaspoon finely grated lemon zest

2 teaspoons fresh lemon juice

½ teaspoon ground cinnamon

¼ teaspoon ground nutmeg

⅛ teaspoon ground cloves

Pinch of salt

streusel topping

½ cup all-purpose flour

¼ cup chopped pecans

¼ cup light brown sugar, loosely packed

½ teaspoon ground cinnamon

Pinch of salt

3 tablespoons unsalted butter, at room temperature, cut into small pieces

Powdered sugar for finishing

continued

Holiday Dried and Fresh Fruit Tartlets (continued)

. . .

To prepare the pastry crust: In a standing mixer with a paddle attachment or in a food processor, mix together the butter, powdered sugar, cinnamon, and salt until smooth. Blend in the egg until smooth. Add the flour and mix until the dough can be pressed into a ball. Press the dough into a flat disk, wrap in plastic film, and refrigerate 30 minutes or until firm enough to roll.

While the pastry chills, prepare the fruit filling: Combine the apple, pear, figs, apricots, currants, and cranberries or cherries in a medium saucepan. Scrape in the seeds of the vanilla bean and add the pod. Stir in the sugar, brandy, lemon zest, lemon juice, cinnamon, nutmeg, cloves, salt, and ¾ cup water. Bring the mixture to a boil, then reduce to a simmer and cook until the dried fruits begin to soften, 5 to 7 minutes. Set aside to cool.

Preheat the oven to 350 degrees F and position a rack near the center. Place six 4-inch fluted tart pans with removable bottoms or similar size molds on a rimmed baking sheet. Roll the pastry ⅛ inch thick on a floured surface using a floured rolling pin. Use an inverted tart pan to cut six rounds

that are slightly larger than the top of the pan. Press the rounds firmly into the bottoms and sides of the pans, patching any tears. Bake the tart shells until they are light golden brown, about 15 minutes. Leave the oven on.

While the pastry bakes, prepare the streusel topping: Stir together the flour, pecans, brown sugar, cinnamon, and salt in a medium bowl. Add the butter and rub with your fingertips until it is well distributed and the mixture has the texture of cookie crumbs. Set aside.

Remove and discard the vanilla pod from the fruit. Use a slotted spoon to strain the fruit and fill the tart shells. (You might have a few tablespoons of syrup left to drizzle over the finished tarts or to enjoy over ice cream.) Distribute the streusel topping over the fruit filling. Bake the tarts on the baking sheet until they are light golden brown, about 25 minutes. Cool the tarts 10 minutes before carefully removing them from their pans. Dust with powdered sugar and serve warm or at room temperature.

makes 6 servings

Caramel Apricot Pecan Tart

• • •

This gorgeous tart combines a pecan crust, a sticky-sweet caramel pecan filling studded with dried apricots, and a crumble topping. Both you and your guests will be dazzled by your ability to easily master such a scrumptious and sophisticated dessert.

MAKING THE MATCH

Sherry (even the ultra-sweet Pedro Ximénez), malmsey Madeira, and Australian muscat all match well with the caramel, nut, and dried fruit flavors in this tart. Botrytised wines and apricots are a great match, making wines from the Sauternes region or a Tokaji 5 or 6 puttonyos good options. We love this with Isabel Estate Noble Sauvage (Marlborough, New Zealand), made from botrytis-affected sauvignon blanc grapes.

pecan crust

⅓ cup pecans

⅓ cup granulated sugar

½ cup (1 stick) unsalted butter, at room temperature

½ teaspoon pure vanilla extract

1 large egg white

1¼ cups all-purpose flour

¼ teaspoon salt

topping

1 cup all-purpose flour

⅓ cup light brown sugar, lightly packed

⅓ cup (⅔ stick) unsalted butter, at room temperature

½ teaspoon salt

filling

½ cup (1 stick) unsalted butter

1 cup light brown sugar, lightly packed

¼ cup honey

1¼ cups pecans, coarsely chopped

¼ cup heavy cream

¾ cup dried apricots, coarsely chopped

To make the crust: Preheat the oven to 325 degrees F and position a rack near the center. Toast the pecans until they are golden in the center when you break one in half, about 8 minutes. Cool the nuts completely.

Combine the toasted pecans and granulated sugar in a food processor and grind as finely as possible. Add the butter and vanilla and process until smooth, scraping the bowl as needed. Add the egg white and process until well combined. Add the flour and salt and pulse until the mixture comes together into a ball. Turn the dough out onto a floured surface, knead briefly, then form the dough into a flat disk. Wrap the disk in plastic film and refrigerate 30 minutes or until firm enough to roll.

Preheat the oven to 350 degrees F. With a floured rolling pin, roll the chilled pastry into an 11-inch round on a floured board, moving the dough frequently to prevent it from sticking. Use a flat, rimless baking sheet to transfer the pastry to a 10-inch tart pan. Press the pastry firmly into the bottom and sides of the pan, patching any tears. Roll the pin firmly over the top of the pan to neatly trim the edge. Bake until golden brown, about 25 minutes. Transfer to a rack to cool, leaving the oven on.

While the crust bakes, make the topping and filling: For the topping, combine the flour, brown sugar, butter, and salt in a small bowl. Use your fingertips to incorporate the butter into the dry ingredients until it forms a crumbly dough. Set aside.

For the filling, heat and stir the butter, brown sugar, and honey in a heavy medium saucepan until the butter melts and the mixture comes to a full boil. Boil for 1 minute, then remove the pan from the heat and add the chopped pecans and cream. (Take care, as it will sputter and steam.) Wait 30 seconds for the steam to subside, then stir to combine.

Sprinkle the chopped apricots over the bottom of the baked crust. Pour the filling over the apricots and bake the tart for 10 minutes. Sprinkle the crumble mixture evenly over the top, then return the tart to the oven until the surface is bubbling, about 20 minutes longer. Transfer the tart to a rack to cool. Cut the tart with a thin, long, sharp knife, dipping the knife in hot water and wiping it clean between slices.

makes 12 servings

Chocolate Currant Tartlets

. . .

These buttery, flaky tartlets sport a soft, warm filling studded with brandy-soaked currants. For deep, dark chocolate flavor, it's worth splurging on the best chocolate, such as Callebaut, Valrhona, or Guittard, with 64 to 72 percent cocoa mass.

MAKING THE MATCH

The chocolate and brandied currants pair well with traditional ports as well as fortified wines made from non-traditional grapes, such as a cabernet sauvignon port. Late harvest zinfandel, Banyuls, or Maury also match well. We enjoy these with Domaine La Tour Vieille Banyuls (France).

1 cup dried currants

½ cup brandy

pastry crust

½ cup (1 stick) unsalted butter, at room temperature

¼ cup powdered sugar

⅛ teaspoon salt

1¼ cups all-purpose flour

filling

2 large eggs

¼ cup granulated sugar

4 ounces bittersweet chocolate, melted (see page 34)

Combine the currants and brandy in a small bowl; set aside. Preheat the oven to 350 degrees F and position a rack in the lower third of the oven. Place eight 3-inch tartlet molds or ramekins onto a rimmed baking sheet.

To make the pastry crust: Mix the butter and powdered sugar until smooth in the bowl of a standing mixer using the paddle attachment. Stir the salt into the flour, add to the butter, and mix just until you can press the dough into a ball with your hands. (This can also be mixed by hand or in a food processor.) Press a small piece of dough firmly into the bottom and sides of the molds, trimming the tops to even them. Bake the tart shells until light golden brown, 12 to 15 minutes, pressing down on the shells if they puff. Transfer the pan to a rack to cool. Leave the oven on.

While the tart shells bake, make the filling: Whip the eggs and granulated sugar on high speed until they are pale and light, about 5 minutes. Stir in the melted chocolate. Use a slotted spoon to strain the currants, reserving the liquid, and add half of the currants to the chocolate mixture. Stir in up to 2 tablespoons of the soaking liquid, to taste. Reserve remaining currants and brandy for garnish.

Distribute the filling among the baked tart shells. Return the baking sheet with the filled tarts to the oven and bake until the filling is set and slightly puffed around the edges and a dark, shiny circle about the size of a quarter remains in the center of each tartlet, 10 to 12 minutes. Allow the tarts to cool at least 15 minutes before carefully removing them from their pans. The tarts are best served warm but can also be served at room temperature. Top with a spoonful of the reserved currants and a drizzle of the brandy soaking liquid.

makes 8 servings

Apricot, Cherry, and Pistachio Biscotti

• • •

The word *biscotti* is derived from the Italian words for "twice" (bis) and "cooked" (cotto). A second baking dries the cookies, increasing their keeping power and making them perfect for dunking. With a gorgeous jeweled appearance and an open grain, this version just begs to be dunked in its traditional Italian mate—vin santo. These are great with a bowl of ice cream, or as part of an assorted cookie plate.

MAKING THE MATCH

These cookies are an excellent match with a vin santo such as the Fattoria Montellori Vin Santo Bianco dell'Empolese (Tuscany, Italy), a wine long on nuts with a citrus peel finish. They are also wonderful with other late harvest white wines with complementary apricot flavors, a sweet oloroso or cream sherry, or a ruby port to bring out the cherries.

1½ cups all-purpose flour

⅓ cup sugar

1½ teaspoons baking powder

¼ teaspoon salt

2 large eggs

1½ teaspoons pure vanilla extract

½ cup dried apricots, coarsely chopped

½ cup dried cherries, coarsely chopped

¼ cup shelled pistachios, toasted and coarsely chopped (see page 139)

Preheat the oven to 325 degrees F and position a rack near the center. Line a baking sheet with parchment paper or a silicone baking mat. Sift together the flour, sugar, baking powder, and salt; set aside.

Beat the eggs at high speed using a handheld electric mixer or a standing mixer with a whisk attachment until they are very light and foamy, about 4 minutes. Add the vanilla. Mix in the flour mixture at low speed until incorporated, then the apricots, cherries, and pistachios. (The batter will be very stiff, so you may want to do the final mixing with your hands.)

Turn the dough out onto a lightly floured surface and knead once or twice to form a ball. Divide the dough into thirds and form each into a log approximately 1½ inches across. Space the logs 1 inch apart on the baking sheet and bake until firm and light brown, about 25 minutes. Transfer the logs to a flat surface and cool 10 minutes. Reduce the oven to 275 degrees F.

With a serrated knife, using a sawing motion, cut the logs at a slight angle into slices ¼ to ½ inch thick. Lay the cookies flat on the baking sheet and bake until they are dry to the touch and beginning to color, about 25 minutes. Transfer the cookies to racks and cool completely. (They can be stored in an airtight container at room temperature for up to 1 month.)

makes about 30 biscotti

Creamy Risotto Pudding with Brandied Figs

. . .

Arborio rice and whipped cream make for a luxuriously rich yet surprisingly light rice pudding. Lowfat milk helps make up for the splurge—it's actually preferred here because the rice absorbs it more easily than whole milk. Use any white or golden figs in this recipe; common varieties are Calimyrna and Kalamata. The figs can be served warm, chilled, or at room temperature.

MAKING THE MATCH

The rich, creamy texture of this pudding calls for a medium- to full-bodied wine. We love this with the dried fruit flavors of brandy-fortified Merryvale Vineyards Antigua Muscat De Frontignan (Napa Valley, California). Other muscats or Banyuls also match well. Or substitute port (but not tawny port) for the brandy in the figs and serve the dessert with the same port.

brandied figs

One 6-inch vanilla bean, split lengthwise

6 ounces dried white figs, cut crosswise into ½-inch-thick slices (about 1½ cups sliced)

⅓ cup brandy

1 tablespoon sugar

1 teaspoon finely grated lemon zest

pudding

½ cup arborio or carnaroli rice

3 to 4 cups lowfat (1% or 2%) milk

⅓ cup sugar

Pinch of salt

½ cup heavy cream

To make the brandied figs: Scrape the seeds from half the vanilla bean into a small saucepan. (Reserve the other half for the pudding.) Drop the scraped pod into the pot and add the figs, brandy, 1 tablespoon sugar, lemon zest, and ½ cup water. Bring the mixture to a boil over high heat, stirring, then reduce the heat to low and simmer gently, stirring occasionally, until the figs soften and the liquid is thick and syrupy, 20 to 30 minutes. Add water, if needed, to keep the mixture saucy. Cool the figs to room temperature, then cover and refrigerate. (The figs can be refrigerated for up to 3 days.)

While the figs simmer, prepare the pudding: Combine the rice, 3 cups milk, the ⅓ cup sugar, and salt in a wide, heavy saucepan. Scrape in the seeds from the reserved half of the vanilla bean and add the pod. Bring the mixture to a boil over high heat, stirring constantly with a wooden spoon. Reduce the heat to medium to keep it at a lively bubble and cook, stirring occasionally, until the rice has absorbed

most of the milk and is tender but retains some texture, about 25 minutes. Add up to 1 cup of milk as the rice simmers to keep the pudding soupy; it will thicken further as it cools.

Transfer the pudding to a bowl to cool. When it is near room temperature, press plastic film directly onto the surface of the pudding and refrigerate until cold, at least 1 hour or up to 1 week.

To serve, remove the vanilla bean pods from both the rice and the figs. In a medium bowl, whip the cream to medium peaks. Fold in the rice mixture and then spoon the pudding into dessert cups, topping each with brandied figs just before serving.

makes 6 servings

CREAM

Given the opportunity, most people will spread
butter on a croissant that already contains
plenty of it. They will top pudding with a dollop
of whipped cream, or a rich cake with a scoop
of ice cream. Is this gilding the lily? Or does the
combination somehow add up to more than
the sum of its parts? § Some might imagine
the combination of a rich custard with an opulent
full-bodied wine to be over the top. In our
experience the opposite is true. The right wine
can tame a dessert, preventing its richness from
becoming overbearing. Continually moving
between dessert and wine keeps the experience
exciting. The wine refreshes the palate, preparing
it for another bite. The next bite of dessert cries
out for another sip. It is a match made in heaven.

God's always got a custard pie up his sleeve.

— MARGARET FORSTER, BRITISH SCREENWRITER

For this reason, we do not shy away from pairing these indulgences with the most luxurious dessert wines. There's no doubt that a rich dessert can sometimes benefit from a crisp, palate-cleansing wine, perhaps with some effervescence, so long as the wine is at least as sweet as the dessert. The wine's acidity keeps both wine and dessert from becoming cloying. But these desserts are at their best with wines that can match their plush, mouth-filling texture: sweet sherries, malmsey Madeiras, beerenausleses or trockenbeerenausleses, ice wines, and French and Australian fortified muscats.

Sour Cream Butter Cake

• • •

This variation on the traditional pound cake is buttery rich with a delicate crumb. Sour cream makes it extra moist. For the best texture, be sure to bring the butter, eggs, and sour cream to room temperature. We recommend using a high quality butter for this cake (see page 28).

MAKING THE MATCH

A cream sherry is an excellent match for this cake; the wine brings the butter forward in the dessert while the cake brings out caramel flavors in the sherry. A muscat, orange muscat, or a late harvest riesling with some botrytis are also good choices. You don't want to overwhelm the cake with an extremely sweet, viscous wine, nor do you want to forget its richness with something too light. We especially like this with Campbells Rutherglen Tokay (Australia).

Butter and all-purpose flour for pans

3 cups cake flour

¾ teaspoon baking powder

¾ teaspoon baking soda

½ teaspoon salt

1½ cups sugar

1¼ cups (2½ sticks) unsalted butter, at room temperature

2 teaspoons pure vanilla extract

5 large eggs, at room temperature

10 ounces (1¼ cups) sour cream, at room temperature

Preheat the oven to 325 degrees F and position a rack near the center. Butter two 8½-by-4½-by-2½-inch metal loaf pans or a 12-cup bundt or tube pan. Dust the pans with all-purpose flour, tapping out any excess.

Sift together the cake flour, baking powder, baking soda, and salt; set aside. Whip the sugar, butter, and vanilla at high speed for 5 minutes until very light and fluffy, scraping down the bowl with a rubber spatula as needed. Add the eggs one at a time, beating 1 minute on high speed and scraping the bowl after each addition. Mix in half the sifted dry ingredients on low speed just until incorporated. Mix in the sour cream until combined, then the remaining dry ingredients until well mixed.

Transfer the batter to the prepared pans and bake until the tops are light golden brown and spring back when you press them lightly with your finger in the center, 45 to 55 minutes. (The bundt or tube cake will take a little longer). The cake will not rise much. Transfer the cakes to a rack and cool completely.

Run a knife around the edges of the cakes and invert them onto a rack, then back onto a serving plate so that the cakes are right side up. With a sharp knife, cut the cakes into slices at least 1 inch thick.

makes 12 servings

Coffee Cream Tart in a Cocoa-Espresso Crust

. . .

Coffee-infused custard and espresso-laced pastry deliver a powerful coffee punch. If you are sensitive to caffeine, substitute decaffeinated coffee in the filling, crust, or both. Evaporated milk, not to be confused with sweetened condensed milk, makes the custard extra-creamy.

MAKING THE MATCH

This tart pairs well with the toasted coffee flavors typically found in oxidized-style and oak-aged fortified wines, such as sherry, tawny port, and malmsey Madeira. We enjoy this matched with the earthy qualities of a vin santo or port, such as Sandeman 20 Year Old Tawny Port (Portugal).

cocoa-espresso crust

½ cup granulated sugar

5 tablespoons unsalted butter, at room temperature

1½ teaspoons instant espresso powder or very finely ground espresso-roast coffee beans

¼ teaspoon salt

1 large egg

1⅓ cups all-purpose flour

¼ cup unsweetened cocoa powder

coffee cream filling

½ cup whole coffee beans

1 cup heavy cream

One 5-ounce can (½ cup plus 2 tablespoons) evaporated milk

½ cup dark brown sugar, lightly packed

1 small (4-inch) vanilla bean, split lengthwise

1 large egg

3 large egg yolks

Preheat the oven to 325 degrees F.

To prepare the crust: Using a standing mixer with the paddle attachment, beat the sugar, butter, espresso powder, and salt at medium speed until creamy. Add the egg and mix until well blended, scraping down the bowl with a rubber spatula. At low speed, add the flour and cocoa powder and mix until the dough comes together around the beaters. (Alternatively, use a food processor.)

Turn the dough out onto a floured surface. Roll it with a floured rolling pin into a 10-inch circle, moving the dough frequently and adding flour as needed. Use a flat, rimless baking sheet to transfer the pastry to a 9-inch fluted tart pan with a removable bottom. Press the dough firmly into the pan, patching any tears with dough scraps. Bake the crust for 20 minutes. Set the crust aside, leaving the oven on.

To prepare the filling: Use the bottom of a heavy skillet to crack the coffee beans into large pieces. Transfer the cracked beans to a medium saucepan and stir in the cream, evaporated milk, and brown sugar. Scrape the seeds from the vanilla bean into the cream and add the pod. Heat the cream mixture over high heat, stirring occasionally, until it is very hot but not boiling. Reduce the heat as low as possible, stir well, cover, and leave to infuse for 15 minutes. Cool the mixture until it is near room temperature.

Strain the mixture through a fine-mesh strainer; discard the solids. Whisk the whole egg and egg yolks in a small bowl, then whisk them into the cooled coffee cream. Strain the filling into the crust.

Bake the tart on a baking sheet until the filling begins to puff around the edges and is softly set but jiggles in the center when you shake the pan, 30 to 35 minutes. Transfer the tart to a cooling rack and let cool, about 30 minutes. Remove the tart ring, transfer the tart to a serving platter, and refrigerate until chilled, about 2 hours. To avoid condensation, wait until the tart is completely cold before covering with plastic film.

makes 10 servings

Mascarpone Chocolate Swirl Cheesecake

• • •

With no crust to distract attention from the smooth chocolate and mascarpone filling, this cheesecake is one of our all-time favorites. Baking the cheesecake just until it is set—and no longer—preserves its luxurious creaminess.

MAKING THE MATCH

Look for wines that complement the creamy mascarpone and bittersweet chocolate. A late harvest white wine with plenty of body and just enough acidity to relieve the dessert's richness marries well with it. We enjoy this with Lindemans Griffith Botrytis Late Harvest Sémillon (Australia). It also pairs well with a Madeira or cream sherry, as well as vintage and tawny ports that accentuate the chocolate.

Butter for pan

5 ounces bittersweet chocolate, finely chopped

½ cup boiling water

12 ounces (1½ cups) cream cheese, at room temperature

8 ounces (1 cup) mascarpone cheese, at room temperature

¾ cup sugar

1 tablespoon pure vanilla extract

4 large eggs

Preheat the oven to 300 degrees F and position a rack in the lower third of the oven. Butter the sides only of an 8-inch round cake pan. Line the bottom of the pan with a round of parchment paper, leaving the paper unbuttered. Line a baking pan with sides at least 2 inches high and large enough to hold the cake pan with a folded kitchen towel.

Put the chocolate in a medium bowl and pour the boiling water over it. Whisk until the chocolate is smooth. Set aside.

Beat the cream cheese and mascarpone at low speed in a standing mixer using the paddle attachment, scraping down the sides of bowl often, until the mixture is smooth, about 2 minutes. Add the sugar and vanilla and continue to beat until the mixture is smooth and free of lumps. Add the eggs, one at a time, beating until smooth and scraping down the bowl after each addition. The batter will be thinner than most cheesecake batters.

Whisk about one-third of the cheese mixture into the melted chocolate until it is completely incorporated. Spread about 2 cups of the plain batter evenly into the prepared cake pan, then place dollops of about 1 cup of the chocolate batter randomly on top. Use a dinner knife or spatula to swirl the batters together, taking care to keep the light and dark batters distinct. Continue adding the plain and chocolate batters alternately in the same 2 to 1 ratio, swirling gently after each addition of the chocolate, until all of the batter is used.

Fill a kettle with hot water. Set the cake pan inside the towel-lined pan, then put the nested pans onto the oven rack. Pour the water into the outer pan until it reaches about one-third of the way up the sides of the cake pan, taking care not to splash water into the batter.

Bake until the cheesecake is set around the edges and the center of the cake still jiggles when you gently shake the pan, 60 to 70 minutes. Carefully remove the pans from the oven, then lift out the cake pan from the water bath and set it on a rack to cool for 30 minutes. Refrigerate the cake at least 4 hours or overnight until chilled. (To avoid condensation, wait until it is completely cold before covering tightly with plastic film. It can be refrigerated, tightly covered, for up to 1 week.)

Run a thin, sharp knife around the inside of the pan. Center a dinner plate over the top of the pan and, holding the plate and pan tightly together, carefully invert the cake. If the cheesecake sticks, dip the pan in hot water almost all the way up the side for 1 or 2 seconds, dry it, and try again. Gently peel away the parchment paper, then carefully invert the cake a second time onto a serving plate, right-side up. Smooth the edges of the cake with a palette knife if needed. Cut the cheesecake with a thin, sharp knife, dipping the blade in warm water and wiping it clean between slices.

makes 10 servings

Browned Butter Cheesecake

. . .

Cooked gently beyond melting, butter develops a beautiful golden color and nutty flavor. Serve a tall, thin slice of this elegant cheesecake without garnish to let its delicate taste shine through.

MAKING THE MATCH

This cheesecake is designed to showcase your richest, fullest sweet wine. We like it best with a beerenauslese or trockenbeerenauslese, an Australian muscat, a German or Canadian icewine, or a malmsey Madeira. All of these wines bring out the nutty flavors in the browned butter and the crust. At the other end of the spectrum, a demi-sec Champagne offers palate-cleansing contrast, but even a richer wine should offer enough acidity to refresh the palate between bites. For the best of both worlds, try Inniskillin's unusual sparkling icewine (Niagara Peninsula, Canada).

Butter for the pan

1½ cups finely crushed graham crackers (about 9 cracker sheets)

1 tablespoon plus 1 cup sugar

½ cup (1 stick) unsalted butter, melted

12 ounces (1½ cups) cream cheese, at room temperature

8 ounces (1 cup) sour cream, at room temperature

¼ teaspoon salt

½ cup half-and-half

2 teaspoons fresh lemon juice

2 teaspoons pure vanilla extract

3 large eggs

Preheat the oven to 325 degrees F and position a rack in the lower third of the oven. Butter the sides but not the bottom of a 9-inch springform pan. Line a baking pan with sides at least 2 inches high and large enough to hold the springform pan with a folded kitchen towel.

Toss the graham crackers and 1 tablespoon of the sugar together in a medium bowl. Drizzle with ¼ cup of the melted butter and toss again to coat the crumbs. Use a flat-bottomed glass to pack the crumbs firmly into the bottom of the pan. Bake until the crust is fragrant and beginning to color, 8 to 12 minutes; set aside to cool. Leave the oven on.

While the crust bakes, heat the remaining ¼ cup butter in a small, heavy saucepan over medium-high heat, stirring constantly as it melts and begins to sizzle. In about 1 minute, the butter will begin to brown. When it is densely speckled with chestnut-colored bits (but not at all burned), immediately remove the pan from the heat and pour the butter into a bowl to stop the cooking.

Beat the cream cheese, sour cream, salt, and remaining 1 cup sugar at low speed for 2 minutes using a standing mixer with a paddle attachment. (Be sure to stay at low speed to avoid incorporating air into the mixture, especially after adding the eggs.) Scrape down the sides of the bowl often with a rubber spatula to prevent lumps. Mix in the half-and-half, lemon juice, and vanilla and beat 1 minute longer, again scraping the bowl. Add the eggs one at a time, mixing well and scraping the bowl after each addition. Mix in the cooled brown butter just until blended.

Tightly wrap the bottom and at least halfway up the sides of the crust's pan with a double layer of aluminum foil, taking care to cover any seams. Pour the filling over the crust. Set the cheesecake inside the towel-lined pan. Fill a kettle with hot water. Put the nested pans onto the oven rack and pour hot water into the outer pan until it reaches about one-third of the way up the sides of the inner pan but not above the edge of the foil.

Close the oven door, reduce the oven temperature to 300 degrees F, and bake until the cheesecake is barely set, 70 to 80 minutes. It should jiggle slightly in the center when you shake it. Turn off the oven, open the oven door, and leave the cheesecake inside until it reaches room temperature, about 1 hour. Remove the cheesecake pan

from the water bath. Hold the pan over the sink while removing the aluminum foil to catch any trapped water. Refrigerate the cheesecake in the pan for at least 2 hours. (The cake can be refrigerated for up to 1 week. To avoid condensation, wait until it is completely cold before covering tightly with plastic film.)

Run a knife around the rim of the cheesecake to loosen it, then carefully remove the outer ring. Carefully slide a small baking sheet under the cheesecake to transfer it to a platter, or transfer the cake to the platter with the pan bottom in place. Cut the cheesecake with a thin, sharp knife, dipping the blade in warm water and wiping it clean between slices.

makes 10 servings

Pumpkin Pots de Crème with Candied Pecans

• • •

The warm spices on a smooth pumpkin background in these delicate custards remind us of a crisp fall or winter day. Sweet-salty glazed pecans add a toasty crunch. Substitute an equal quantity of baked and puréed Sugar Pie or other good cooking pumpkin for canned.

MAKING THE MATCH

Look for a wine with brown sugar, honey, or spice flavors and bright acidity to balance the rich custard. We love this with a lightly botrytised white wine such as the Chateau Grillon Sauternes (France). It also pairs well with a 10-year tawny port or a muscat, vin santo, or cream sherry.

pots de crème

1 cup canned pumpkin

½ cup light brown sugar, lightly packed

1 cup light cream

2 large eggs

3 large egg yolks

1 tablespoon molasses

1 teaspoon pure vanilla extract

1 teaspoon ground cinnamon

¼ teaspoon fresh grated nutmeg

¼ teaspoon ground cloves

½ teaspoon salt

candied pecans

½ cup granulated sugar

1 tablespoon maple syrup or honey

¼ teaspoon salt

1 cup coarsely chopped pecans

To make the pots de crème: Preheat the oven to 325 degrees F and position a rack near the center. Lightly oil six 4-ounce ramekins. Have ready a pan that is at least 2 inches deep and large enough to hold the ramekins. Line the pan with a clean kitchen towel and arrange the ramekins evenly in the pan.

In a medium bowl, whisk together the pumpkin, brown sugar, cream, eggs, egg yolks, molasses, vanilla, cinnamon, nutmeg, cloves, and salt. Strain the mixture into a 4-cup glass measure or a bowl with a pouring spout, pressing the mixture through the strainer with a spoon or rubber spatula. Pour the custard into the prepared ramekins.

Fill a kettle with hot water. Place the nested pans on the oven rack and pour hot water into the outer pan until it reaches about halfway up the sides of the ramekins. Cover the pan loosely with aluminum foil and bake until the custards are set but still jiggle when you shake them, 30 to 40 minutes. Reduce the oven temperature to 275 degrees F.

Transfer the pans to a cooling rack and remove the foil, leaving the pots de crème in the water bath until they reach room temperature. Remove the cooled ramekins from the water bath and refrigerate until chilled, about 2 hours. To avoid condensation, wait until they are completely cold before covering tightly with plastic film.

While the pots de crème bake, prepare the pecans: Bring the granulated sugar, maple syrup, salt, and ¼ cup water to a boil, stirring, in a heavy medium saucepan over high heat. Reduce the heat as low as possible and stir in the pecans. Cook the pecans at a slow simmer for 30 minutes, stirring occasionally. Drain the pecans and discard the syrup.

Spread the pecans on a baking sheet lined with parchment paper or a silicone baking mat and toast them in the oven until they are golden brown, 20 to 25 minutes. To check for doneness, break a pecan in half and look for a golden color inside. Cool the nuts completely on the parchment.

Place the chilled pots de crème on individual serving plates and garnish with candied pecans. Serve additional pecans in a bowl on the side.

makes 6 servings

CARAMEL, HONEY & SPICE

If not *everything* nice, sugar and spice certainly make for alluring aromas and comforting desserts. Little girls are reputed to be made of them (some more spice than sugar), while adults find delight in pairing them with sweet wines. These flavors are especially captivating in brisk weather, when toasty spices provide welcome warmth. § This chapter brings together the cooked sugar flavor of caramel, the fragrant honey barrel, and the spice box. In pairing them with wines, the trick is to play up that sweet and spicy bouquet without overwhelming the wine. In some cases, wines themselves contribute caramel flavors from dried fruit or oxidation, honey from concentrated sugar and botrytis, and spice flavors, including notes of pepper, cinnamon, or ginger. Gewürztraminer is named for its spicy nature (*gewürz* is German for spice). Desserts with these flavors help to coax out the same elements in a wine.

THE WINE LOVER'S DESSERT COOKBOOK

Brown sugar lassie,
Caramel treat,
Honey-gold baby
Sweet enough to eat.

— LANGSTON HUGHES, "HARLEM SWEETIES"

Fortified wines boasting full-bodied flavor tend to pair well with the desserts in this chapter. With their oxidized nuttiness, sweet sherry and Madeira make good matches, as do certain ports. Botrytised wines harmonize with these desserts, as do honey-sweet ice wines. Muscats, especially fortified styles, synchronize beautifully with honey. Look for the less common brown muscat of Australia, with soft hints of cinnamon, or black muscat, which can bring out hidden nuances of caramel, nuts, and spice. Select a wine that matches or exceeds the dessert's sweetness and that has enough body to hold up to the dessert's intense flavors and sometimes substantial texture.

Brown Sugar and Cinnamon Crème Brûlée

. . .

For this dessert, we use heavy cream and egg yolks for a silky custard that perfectly contrasts with the crackling caramelized sugar top. Use cream with no additives to ensure that the custard will set up properly.

MAKING THE MATCH

This dessert pairs beautifully with a malmsey Madeira, a cream sherry, or a rich muscat such as the Yalumba Museum Old Sweet White Barossa NV Muscat (South Australia). It is also a natural with a botrytised riesling with marmalade and spice flavors to complement the custard and the caramelized sugar topping

- 1 large egg
- 3 large egg yolks
- 2 cups heavy cream (see page 28)
- ⅓ cup brown sugar, lightly packed
- ½ teaspoon ground cinnamon
- 1 small (4-inch) vanilla bean, split lengthwise
- 3 to 4 tablespoons granulated sugar

Preheat the oven to 325 degrees F and position a rack in the lower third of the oven. Have ready a pan that is at least 2 inches deep and large enough to hold 4 wide, shallow crème brûlée dishes or 6-ounce ramekins. Line the bottom of the pan with a folded kitchen towel. Arrange the ramekins evenly on the towel in the pan.

Whisk the whole egg and egg yolks briefly in a medium bowl. Whisk in the cream, brown sugar, and cinnamon until well blended. Scrape the seeds from the vanilla bean into the cream mixture and mix well. Strain the mixture through a fine-mesh strainer into a 4-cup glass measure or a bowl with a pouring spout. Divide the custard among the ramekins.

Fill a kettle with hot water. Place the baking pan with the ramekins onto the oven rack and carefully pour water into the pan until it reaches about halfway up the ramekins. Drape a single piece of aluminum foil loosely over all the ramekins. Bake until the custards are softly set but jiggle when you shake the pan, 35 to 40 minutes. (Custard in deeper ramekins may take longer.) If some set before others, carefully transfer them to a cooling rack with an oven mitt or sturdy tongs.

Transfer the custards to a rack and cool for 30 minutes, then refrigerate until chilled and set, about 2 hours or up to 3 days. To avoid condensation, wait until they are completely cold before covering tightly with plastic film.

Just before serving, sprinkle 2 to 3 teaspoons of granulated sugar evenly over each custard. (Wide ramekins will require more sugar than narrow ones.) Holding a propane kitchen torch with the flame about 2 inches from the top of one of the custards, move it slowly and steadily over the surface until the sugar melts and browns, about 2 minutes. Repeat with the others. If you do not have a torch, preheat the broiler, positioning its rack as close as possible to the heating element. Place the ramekins on a rimmed baking sheet and broil the custards, watching and checking frequently until the sugar is melted and starting to brown, 2 to 7 minutes. Serve immediately or within 1 hour.

makes 4 servings

Apricot Gingerbread Upside-Down Cake

. . .

Golden apricots lacquered with a shiny brown sugar–glaze make this rustic cake appear quite elegant. If apricots are not in season, substitute a 15-ounce can of apricots packed in light syrup or in their natural juices; drain and pat dry before using.

MAKING THE MATCH

The caramelized sugar and spice flavors in this cake pair well with late harvest botrytised wines. Try pairing this with a Sauternes, riesling, Tokaji, or ice wine. Orange muscat or a lighter style tawny port also works well, and a late harvest gewürztraminer brings out the spices. Our favorite match for this cake is Grgich Hills Violetta (Napa Valley, California), a botrytis-kissed blend of sauvignon blanc, chardonnay, and riesling.

Butter for cake pan

12 tablespoons unsalted butter, at room temperature

¾ cup lightly packed dark brown sugar

6 large or 10 small fresh apricots (about 12 ounces), halved and pitted

2 cups all-purpose flour

2 teaspoons ground ginger

1 teaspoon baking soda

1 teaspoon ground cinnamon

¼ teaspoon ground cloves

½ teaspoon salt

⅔ cup molasses

⅓ cup granulated sugar

1 large egg

¾ cup boiling water

Preheat the oven to 350 degrees F and position a rack near the center. Butter the sides only of a 9-by-2-inch round cake pan.

Melt 6 tablespoons butter with the brown sugar in a small, deep saucepan over medium heat, stirring occasionally until the butter is melted. Reduce heat to low and leave undisturbed for 3 to 4 minutes to melt the sugar. Stir slowly at first to avoid sloshing the butter, then more briskly, until the butter and sugar blend together into a smooth caramel. Pour the hot caramel into the prepared pan, tilting to coat the bottom. Arrange the apricots cut-side down in a decorative pattern over the caramel. Set the pan aside.

Sift together the flour, ginger, baking soda, cinnamon, cloves, and salt; set aside. In a medium bowl, mix the molasses, granulated sugar, and remaining 6 tablespoons butter on high speed until light, about 2 minutes, scraping down the bowl as needed. Add the egg and beat another minute. (The mixture may look separated.) On low speed,

mix in half of the flour mixture just until incorporated. Beat in the boiling water on low speed. Mix in the remaining flour mixture just until combined.

Pour the batter over the apricots in the pan, using a spatula to coax the batter between the fruits and to smooth the top. Bake just until the top feels firm at the center when lightly pressed and a toothpick inserted near the center comes out clean, 35 to 40 minutes. Transfer to a rack and cool for 10 to 15 minutes.

While the cake is still warm, run a sharp, thin knife around the inside of the pan. Place a large serving plate over the top of the pan and, holding the pan and plate tightly together, invert the cake onto the plate. Carefully remove the cake pan, spooning any remaining caramel over the cake. This cake is delicious warm from the oven, but is also very good at room temperature.

makes 8 servings

Crostata di Ricotta (Honey Ricotta Tart)

• • •

Tarts filled with sweetened ricotta cheese are a traditional dessert in Sicily and are also popular in Rome. We've added cornmeal to the crust and honey to the filling for crunchy contrast and earthy flavors that pair nicely with many late harvest wines.

MAKING THE MATCH

The abundant earthy and dairy flavors in this tart call for a medium-bodied wine with notes of honey and orange blossom. It pairs well with both ice wine and vin santo. Orange muscat brings out the tart's subtle orange flavor, while the delicious Chateau des Charmes Late Harvest Riesling (Niagara Peninsula, Canada) beautifully accentuates the tart's honey and citrus undertones.

pastry crust

½ cup (1 stick) unsalted butter, at room temperature

3 tablespoons sugar

1 large egg yolk

¼ teaspoon salt

1 cup all-purpose flour

⅓ cup fine cornmeal

ricotta filling

15 ounces (1¾ cups) whole milk ricotta cheese

3 ounces (⅓ cup) cream cheese, at room temperature

½ cup heavy cream

¼ cup sugar

2 large eggs

1 large egg yolk

2 tablespoons honey

1 tablespoon finely grated orange zest

2 teaspoons pure vanilla extract

To make the crust: Process the butter, 3 tablespoons sugar, egg yolk, and salt in a food processor, scraping down the bowl with a spatula as needed. Add the flour and cornmeal and pulse just until combined. Turn the dough out onto a floured surface and knead 2 to 3 times to bring the dough together into a ball. Press the dough into a flat disk, wrap in plastic film, and refrigerate until firm, about 30 minutes or up to 3 days.

Preheat the oven to 350 degrees F and position a rack near the center. Briefly knead the dough on a floured surface, then roll it into a 12-inch round, keeping the work surface, dough, and rolling pin well floured and moving the dough frequently to prevent it from sticking. Work quickly, handling the dough as little as possible to keep it cool.

Use a flat, rimless baking sheet to transfer the pastry to a 10-inch fluted tart pan with a removable bottom, draping the pastry over the pan to center it. Push the pastry firmly into the bottom and sides of the pan, using dough scraps to patch any tears. If you find this soft dough difficult to work with, either chill it again or press pieces of the dough into place in the pan. Roll the pin firmly over the top of the pan to neatly trim the edge. Bake the crust for 20 minutes; it will not be fully baked. Set the pan on a rack to cool. Leave the oven on.

While the dough bakes, make the filling: Pulse the ricotta, cream cheese, cream, ¼ cup sugar, eggs, egg yolk, honey, orange zest, and vanilla in a food processor until completely smooth.

Pour the filling into the partially baked crust and bake until the filling is set, with golden brown spots dotting the surface, 35 to 40 minutes. Transfer the pan to a rack to cool until it is room temperature. When it is cool, remove the sides of the pan and transfer the tart with the base to a serving platter. Cut the crostata into wedges with a sharp knife and serve at room temperature.

makes 10 servings

Honeyed Fig Tart

• • •

This tart is especially attractive with a mix of green figs such as Kadota or Calimyrna varieties, and black figs such as Mission or Brown Turkey, which range in color from brown to purple-black. It is delicious served with a dollop of thick Greek-style whole-milk yogurt, sweetened with honey.

MAKING THE MATCH

Vin santo brings out the earthy flavors of honey and fig in this tart. Taylor Fladgate 10 Year Tawny Port (Portugal) is a lovely match for the dessert's sweet, nutty, and caramelized flavors. Cream sherry or Madeira also match well.

⅓ cup plus ¼ cup hazelnuts, toasted and skinned (see page 139)

5 tablespoons sugar

5 tablespoons unsalted butter, at room temperature

1 large egg

1¼ cups all-purpose flour

½ teaspoon baking powder

½ teaspoon ground cinnamon

¼ teaspoon salt

2 pint baskets figs (about 5 cups), preferably a mix of black and green, stemmed

⅓ cup heavy cream

¼ cup mild-flavored honey

Pulse ⅓ cup hazelnuts with the sugar in a food processor until they are the texture of cookie crumbs. Add the butter and process, scraping down the work bowl as needed, until creamy. Add the egg and mix until combined. Sift together the flour, baking powder, cinnamon, and salt. Add to the butter mixture and process until the dough comes together in a ball. Wrap the dough in plastic film, pressing to form a flat disk, and chill until firm, at least 30 minutes.

Preheat the oven to 350 degrees F and position a rack in the lower third of the oven. Place the chilled dough on a floured surface and pat it in several places with a rolling pin to soften it. Roll the dough with a floured rolling pin into a 12-inch circle, moving the dough frequently to prevent it from sticking. Use a flat, rimless baking sheet to transfer the pastry to a 10-inch tart pan with a removable bottom. Press the pastry snugly into the bottom and sides, patching any tears with your fingers. Roll the pin firmly over the top of the pan to neatly trim the edge. Bake the tart shell until it is light golden brown, about 20 minutes. Leave the oven on.

While the crust bakes, reserve a few of the smallest, ripest figs and cut the remaining ones into different sizes; some in quarters, others in halves. Crush the remaining ¼ cup hazelnuts into large, uneven pieces with the back of a chef's knife or the bottom of a heavy skillet. Warm the cream and honey in a large saucepan over medium heat until the honey is melted. Add all of the figs and the hazelnuts, stirring gently to coat them.

Pour the filling into the baked tart shell, distributing the figs evenly. Bake until the crust is a shade darker and the figs are warm and shiny, about 20 minutes longer. Serve hot from the oven or at room temperature.

makes 8 servings

Wine Lovers' Caramels

• • •

Caramels made with the rarified French sea salt, *fleur de sel*, have long been a favorite in Brittany and are becoming increasingly popular here. We make these supple, buttery caramels with the widely available gray salt of Brittany, but any sea salt with good, clean flavor and no additives will work. Caramels involve some precision but they are not difficult and are well worth the effort.

MAKING THE MATCH

These rich caramels—with their bitter, mineral, and salt notes—amplify the subtlest flavors in fine dessert wines. They are sublime with a glass of Sauternes, trockenbeerenauslese, or other botrytis-affected wine, and pair nicely with a rich, sweet sherry or malmsey Madeira. When we can find it, we love them with Gsellmann & Gsellmann Trockenbeerenauslese from Burgenland, Austria.

Butter for the waxed paper

1 cup light cream

¾ teaspoon gray salt, fleur de sel, or coarse sea salt

½ teaspoon pure vanilla extract

2 cups sugar

⅓ cup light corn syrup

½ cup (1 stick) unsalted butter, at room temperature, cut into 8 pieces

Line an 8-inch square metal baking pan with waxed paper, laying strips in two directions so that flaps extend beyond the edge of the pan on all sides. (This will help you lift out the caramel after it sets.) Butter the paper. Place the pan on a cooling rack.

Stir together the cream, salt, and vanilla in a small saucepan and heat until the mixture comes to a simmer. Turn off the heat and leave the pan on the stovetop.

Heat the sugar and corn syrup in a deep, wide, heavy 4-quart saucepan over medium heat, stirring frequently with a wooden spatula, until the sugar is completely dissolved, 15 to 20 minutes. To prevent the formation of sugar crystals, periodically wash down the sides of the pan with a clean pastry brush dipped in cold water.

Increase the heat to medium-high and boil without disturbing —swirl occassionally if needed but do not stir—until a candy thermometer registers 300 degrees F. (If you don't have a candy thermometer, drop a small spoonful of the caramel into a glass of ice-cold water; when cool, it should form brittle threads that break when you try to bend them.)

Swirl in the butter, then take the caramel off the heat and carefully pour in the cream in a slow stream; it will sputter and steam for about 30 seconds. Return the caramel to medium heat and continue to cook, swirling or stirring with a clean wooden spatula only as needed, until the thermometer registers 248 to 250 degrees F, 15 minutes longer. (To test, drop a small spoonful of the caramel into ice-cold water; when cool, it should form a firm ball that holds its shape but flattens when you gently squeeze it.)

Remove the thermometer and pour the caramel into the lined baking pan. Do not scrape the bottom of the saucepan, to avoid dislodging any sugar crystals. Leave the caramel absolutely undisturbed until it is completely cool and set, about 4 hours.

Using the waxed paper flaps, pull the caramel from the pan and invert it onto a second piece of waxed paper on a flat surface. If it is stubborn, place the pan over low heat for a few seconds to loosen it. Peel off the waxed paper and use a sharp, heavy knife or pizza wheel to cut

the caramels into 8 strips in one direction, then 8 in the other. If the knife sticks to the caramel, run the blade under hot water or oil it lightly.

Wrap each caramel in a 4-inch square of waxed paper or cellophane, twisting the ends tightly in opposite directions. Store the caramels in an airtight container in a cool, dry place for up to 1 week.

makes 64 caramels

Caramel Tips

* Make these on a cool, dry day, as heat and especially humidity can interfere with successful candy making. In warm weather, cook the caramel on the firmer side during the second cooking, about 250 degrees, to keep it firm at room temperature.

* For the smoothest caramels, wait until the sugar is completely dissolved before inserting a thermometer, and wash utensils well between stirring and dipping into the caramel. Metal utensils tend to encourage the formation of crystals that can make caramels grainy; we suggest using a wooden spatula.

* Avoid pans coated with tin or nonstick linings, as hot caramel can melt them. Glazed cast iron retains too much heat and can easily burn the caramel.

* Take care when working with sugar at high temperatures. use oven mitts and reduce spattering by pouring the cream through an inverted large strainer into the hot caramel.

* Keep a bowl of ice water by the stove to check the stage of caramel, or to quickly cool the bottom of the pan and stop the cooking.

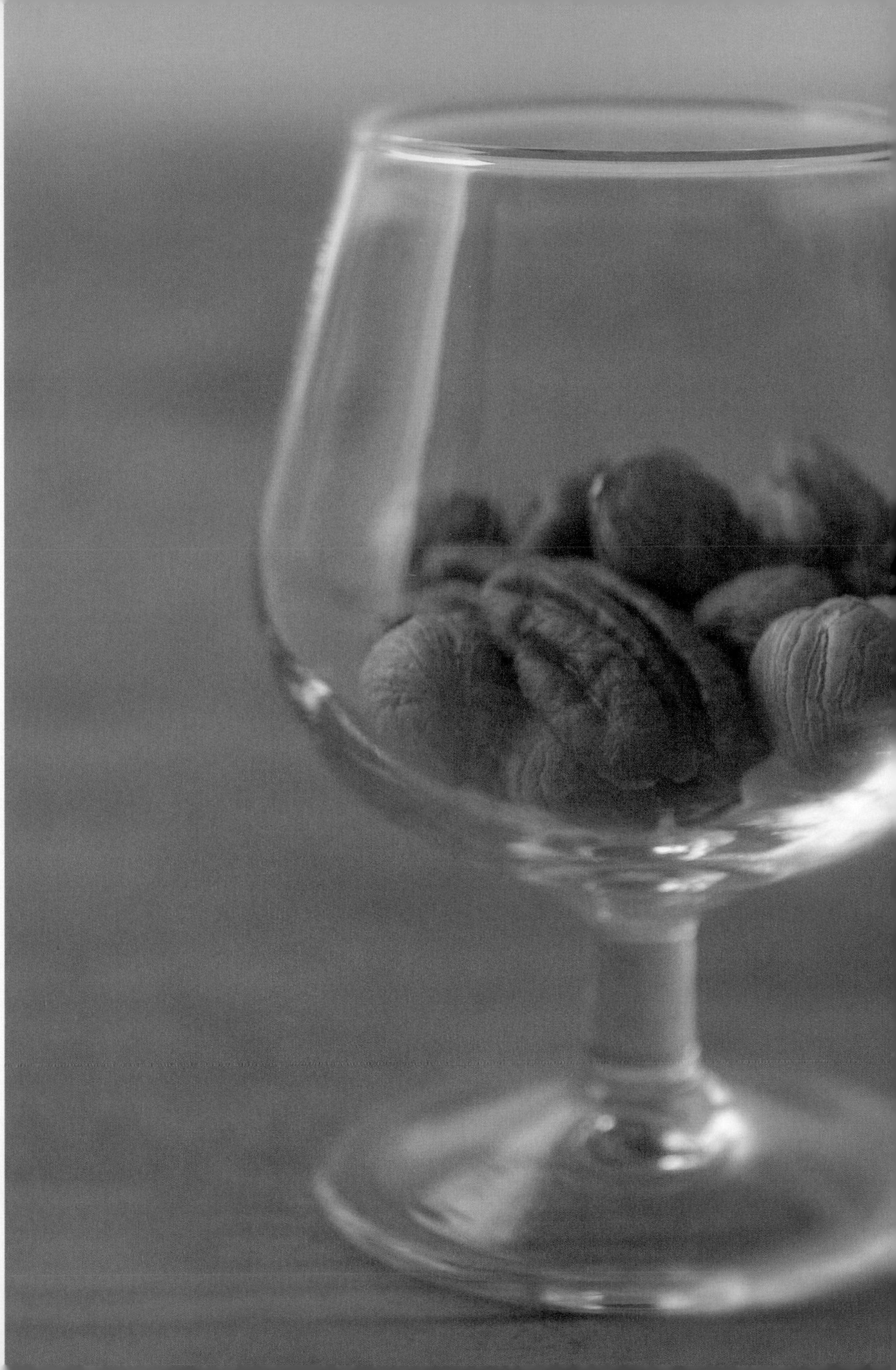

NUTS

While nuts are an embellishment in some desserts, in this chapter they take center stage. Nuts are a classic pairing with wine, both dry and sweet. Fortified wines, in particular, often taste of almonds, hazelnuts, or walnuts. § Nuts can act as a bridge ingredient, helping to seal the match between the wine and other flavors in the dessert. Belonging to the rose family, almonds are one of two hundred species in the genus *Prunus*, along with stone fruits such as apricots, cherries, and peaches. It's no wonder that many of these fruits are so compatible with the nut. Sherry has a special affinity for almonds owing to oxidation in the winemaking process, which imparts nutty flavors and aromas. In Spain it is customary to snack on the two together. Hazelnuts, rich and buttery with a hint of sweetness, are a classic pairing with chocolate. Walnuts impart complexity from the tannins in their papery skins, and become rich, crumbly, and deeply flavorful when toasted. § You will find fortified wines—sherry, Madeira, and port—heavily represented among our pairings with these nutty desserts. Other well-suited wines include those from the Loire based on the chenin blanc grape (Vouvray and Coteaux du Layon are examples), Jurançon from the southwest of France,

The morns are meeker than they were,

The nuts are getting brown;

The berry's cheek is plumper,

The rose is out of town.

— EMILY DICKINSON, "LIFE"

and Sauternes and other botrytised wines. Vin santo is, of course, the quintessential wine for dipping nut-studded biscotti.

Pedro Ximénez, also known as PX, is used primarily to sweeten dry oloroso sherries, transforming them into sweet cream sherries. Served as a wine in its own right, the sugary viscosity of PX would overwhelm most desserts, but we find it superb with Caramel Macadamia Tart, the richest of the lot.

selecting nuts

Although nuts remain freshest in their natural protective covering, shelling them for recipes can be hard work. Always purchase the freshest nuts, shelled or unshelled, that you can find. They should look plump, taste sweet, and be free of any mold or dark spots. Buying them in bulk can allow you to sample one. Be sure to check the freshness dates on packaged nuts for the best flavor. Whole nuts stay fresh longer, so whenever possible, purchase and store them whole and chop them as needed.

With their high levels of oil, nuts require some care to prevent them from turning rancid. Store nuts in an airtight container in the freezer to preserve their flavor and extend their shelf life. When a recipe calls for toasted nuts, toast them shortly before using them for maximum flavor.

Toasting and Grinding Nuts. Spread nuts in a single layer on a rimmed baking sheet and toast at 350 degrees F until they smell fragrant, darken slightly, and feel crisp inside when you bite or break into one. This will take 8 to 12 minutes depending on the type of nut. Shake or stir them occasionally for even cooking. Toasting nuts to a deep golden brown gives them more flavor, but take care not to burn them, as they can turn bitter.

Although oven toasting is the best way to brown nuts evenly, you may also toast them on the stovetop. Place the nuts in a single layer in a cast-iron skillet and toast them over low heat, watching carefully and stirring often.

Hazelnuts require special care because of their clinging skins. Wrap just-toasted hazelnuts in a clean tea towel and rub vigorously to remove most of their skins.

You will be able to grind nuts more finely if they are cold. To cool toasted nuts quickly, spread them on a flat plate or pan, and then place them in the freezer. Grind well-cooled nuts with a small amount of granulated sugar from the recipe to help prevent them from turning to nut butter.

Almond Apricot Pithiviers

• • •

This exquisite domed pastry is named for an ancient town in the Loire Valley, where the classic combination of ultra-flaky pastry and rich almond filling is a local specialty. Our version includes apricots and uses a quick version of puff pastry (sometimes called rough puff or blitz pastry) that cuts a daylong effort down to a few hours. In a pinch, purchase a pound of puff pastry in two large sheets from a local bakery, or use good-quality all-butter frozen puff pastry available in the frozen foods section of some supermarkets and specialty food stores.

MAKING THE MATCH

A wine with full body and good acidity will help balance the richness of the dessert, while aromatic notes of apricot and almond will highlight the flavors in the filling. A Vouvray or other late harvest chenin blanc from the Loire is a natural match. An ice wine or Tokaji would also be a good choice. We love this with Freemark Abbey Edelwein Gold (Napa Valley, California), which complements the filling with a hint of honey.

quick puff pastry

2 cups minus 2 tablespoons all-purpose flour

1 cup (2 sticks) cold unsalted butter, cut into ½-inch pieces

1 teaspoon salt

almond filling

½ cup (about 5½ ounces) almond paste

⅓ cup sugar plus additional for finishing

¼ cup (½ stick) unsalted butter, at room temperature

2 large eggs

⅓ cup all-purpose flour

4 fresh apricots, halved and pitted, or 8 apricot halves from one 15-ounce can, drained and patted dry

1 large egg

1 teaspoon cream or water

To prepare the puff pastry: Toss together the flour, cold butter, and salt in a large bowl. Make a well in the center and pour in ⅓ cup ice-cold water. Use your hands to bring the mixture together into a very shaggy ball of dough, adding up to 3 tablespoons cold water, a tablespoon at a time, if needed. The dough will be very ragged with pieces falling away, but fear not—it will come together as you roll it. It should not be at all sticky. For the flakiest dough, keep the butter in distinct pieces rather than smearing it or blending it into the dough.

Turn the dough onto a floured surface and press it into a rough rectangle. Roll the pastry into an 8-by-12-inch rectangle, with a short edge facing you. Use a bench scraper or large spatula to fold the end nearest you about two-thirds of the way toward the top, then fold the top down over it, as if you were folding a letter. Turn the dough 90 degrees so that an open edge is facing you. Repeat for a second turn: Roll the dough into a large rectangle and fold like a letter. Wrap the folded dough in plastic film, mark it with two thumbprints to indicate the two turns, and refrigerate 15 minutes to firm the butter.

Roll and fold the dough two more times to complete the third and fourth turns. Mark the dough with four thumbprints and refrigerate at least 30 minutes before rolling and shaping the pastry. For even more height in the finished pastry, complete two more optional turns,

continued

Almond Apricot Pithiviers (continued)

• • •

for a total of six turns. (The dough can be refrigerated, tightly wrapped, for up to 3 days or frozen for up to 3 months. Thaw in the refrigerator.)

While the pastry chills, prepare the filling: Break up the almond paste with your hands and put it into the bowl of a standing mixer. Add the ⅓ cup sugar and mix with the paddle attachment at medium speed to break up any lumps. (The filling can also be made with a handheld electric mixer or a food processor.) Blend in the room-temperature butter a tablespoon at a time, scraping down the bowl as needed. Beat 1 minute at high speed, checking to be sure the mixture is free of lumps. Add the eggs one at a time, beating until smooth after each one. Mix in the flour at low speed. Set aside.

Cut the dough crosswise in two pieces, just off center, so that one piece is slightly larger than the other. Wrap and refrigerate the larger piece. Roll the smaller piece into a 10-inch circle on a lightly floured surface. Use a pizza wheel or sharp knife to trim it into a neat circle. Lightly dampen an ungreased rimmed baking sheet with a wet hand and transfer the circle to the sheet.

Arrange the apricot halves in the center of the dough, leaving a two-inch border around the edge. (You may have to cut a few to fit.) Mound the filling over the fruit, doming it slightly. Roll the second piece of pastry into an 11-inch circle and trim neatly. In a small bowl, beat the egg and cream. Brush the egg wash on the border of the bottom dough, then center the larger round over the filling. Use the tines of a fork to press and seal the edges together. Cover the Pithiviers with plastic film and refrigerate 1 hour or up to 8 hours before baking.

Preheat the oven to 425 degrees F and position a rack in the lower third of the oven. Etch a decorative pattern into the top of the pastry, taking care to cut only the top layers and not all the way through to the filling. (Half moons radiating from the center to the edge are traditional.) Brush the Pithiviers with the remaining egg wash, avoiding the outer edges, and sprinkle generously with sugar. Cut a half-inch vent through the center of the top crust.

Bake for 10 minutes. Reduce the heat to 375 degrees F and continue baking until the pastry is a deep golden brown, 20 to 30 minutes. Place the pan on a rack to cool for at least 15 minutes before serving warm.

makes 8 servings

Secrets to Making Flaky Puff Pastry. Despite its reputation as one of a pastry chef's most daunting feats, puff pastry dough is quite forgiving and easy to work with. Follow these simple tips and you will be duly proud of your handiwork.

* Keeping the butter cold is essential to creating light, flaky pastry. Start with flour stored in the freezer and very cold butter.

* Keep the pastry cold but not too cold as you work. You want the butter neither to melt into the dough nor to break through it. Work quickly each time you have the dough out of the refrigerator and don't handle it more than necessary. If the butter softens as you work, wrap and refrigerate the dough for 15 minutes before continuing. If the dough is very stiff after chilling, let it soften at room temperature 10 to 15 minutes before rolling.

* Always roll the dough parallel to its longest side, rolling from the middle away from you and then from the middle toward you. Roll with even pressure, letting up as you reach the edges to avoid rolling over the ends of the dough.

* Square off the dough as you work by coaxing the edges into a neat rectangle with a ruler or bench scraper.

* Brush any excess flour off of the dough before starting and after completing each fold.

* Use a sharp knife or pizza wheel to make definitive cuts. Avoid pressing down on the dough or dragging it as you cut it, which can compress the dough and inhibit it from rising.

* Keep the outer edges free of egg wash, which can make the layers of dough stick together, preventing them from rising.

* Moisten the baking sheet before setting the bottom dough round onto it to anchor the dough, encouraging it to puff as it bakes.

Hazelnut Wafers with Cheese and Fruit

• • •

Sweet wines at once contrast and complement the earthy, nutty, and salty flavors found in fine cheeses, especially when served with these nutty, delicately sweetened wafers. Fresh or dried dates, figs, apricots, or grapes make a lovely addition. Our gratitude goes to Laura Werlin, food writer and cheese expert, for suggesting many of the cheeses on the following pages.

MAKING THE MATCH

Botrytised wines, including Jurançon from the southwest of France and Sauternes-style wines, are among the most friendly with cheese. Sharp and pungent blue cheeses are a good match with Sauternes, muscats, and ice wines. Port and Stilton is a classic pairing. Consider pairing cheeses with wines from the same terroir in which the herds have been grazing. An aged goat cheese from the Loire Valley is perfect with a Loire Valley wine such as a demi-sec or moelleux Vouvray, Coteaux du Layon, or Bonnezeaux. The often pricey Quarts de Chaume from that region has a nose of toasted hazelnuts, making it a great match to both the cheese and the wafers.

⅓ cup hazelnuts, toasted and skinned (see page 139)

¼ cup sugar

2 tablespoons all-purpose flour

Pinch of salt

3 large egg whites, lightly beaten

⅓ to ½ pound each of 2 to 3 cheeses (see Sidebar, page 146)

6 to 12 fresh or dried dates or figs

Preheat the oven to 325 degrees F and position a rack near the center. Line a 17-by-12-inch baking sheet with a silicone baking mat or a lightly oiled piece of parchment paper.

Pulse the nuts with the sugar in a food processor until they are the texture of coarse cornmeal with some slightly larger pieces. Transfer the nuts to a medium bowl and stir in the flour and salt. Whisk in the egg whites until well blended. Using an offset spatula, spread the batter thinly and evenly on the silicone mat, covering about two-thirds of the mat's surface. For the crispiest wafers, you should almost be able to see through the batter, and for even browning, avoid thinning it along the edges. Don't be concerned if the nuts poke small holes in the wafer. Bake until the wafer is brown all over, 12 to 15 minutes. Check frequently toward the end, as the wafer can darken and burn quickly.

Invert the pan over a clean, flat surface and remove the pan. Wait 1 minute before carefully peeling the baking mat from the wafer. When it is completely cool, break the wafer into odd-size serving pieces. Store the wafers in an airtight container at room temperature away from moisture, which will soften them.

Arrange the cheeses on a serving platter and surround with the fruit and hazelnut wafers. Alternatively, serve small portions of the cheeses on individual plates with just one or two pieces of fruit and a smaller piece of the wafer; offer additional wafers on the side.

makes 6 servings

continued

Hazelnut Wafers with Cheese and Fruit / Selecting Cheese (continued)

• • •

Selecting Cheese. It can be fun to offer three very different styles on a cheese plate, allowing guests to experience how each alters the experience of the wine and vice versa. One way is to include a goat's, a cow's, and a sheep's milk cheese. Another is to include a soft, rich cheese; a firmer cheese; and a blue cheese. Below are a few of our favorites for pairing with sweet wines. If there is a good cheese shop in your area, tell them about your wine selections and ask for their suggestions.

Laura Werlin recommends full-flavored, aged cheeses for pairing with sweet wines. Consider a manchego from Spain, an aged goat cheese or gouda (cow or goat), or a Dry Jack from Vella Cheese Company in Sonoma, California, a nutty, almost sweet take on aged Monterey Jack with a rind rubbed dark with black pepper and cocoa. Roth Käse in Wisconsin makes a cow's milk Gruyère that is heat-treated but not pasteurized, preserving the milk's subtle flavors. Washed rind cheeses often have well-developed flavors. Consider a French Reblochon or Epoisses, a rich Italian Taleggio, or an Alsatian Muenster.

Ossau-Iraty is a ewe's milk cheese with a firm but creamy texture and nutty flavor. This cheese is made in the western Pyrenees, in Basque country, handcrafted by shepherds. In its home area, the cheese goes by the nickname, "farmer's dessert." Or try California-based Bellwether Farms' San Andreas, a mild, smooth sheep's milk cheese named for the earthquake fault that runs through the family's property.

Fermier cheeses are made in very small batches using only milk from the cheesemaker's own herd. Lingot de Quercy, one of only a few fermier cheeses available in the United States, is a goat's milk cheese from the French Pyrenees. It is visually striking, with a rind that falls in folds around a runny outer layer encasing a creamy white center. Crottin de Chavignol is a good choice from the Loire Valley. Banon is an attractive goat cheese (often with small amounts of cow's and sheep's milk) that offers rich flavor and smooth texture when ripe. The northern Provençal cheese comes in small wheels washed in eau-de-vie, cured in chestnut or grape leaves, and tied with raffia. Capriole Farms in Indiana makes an American Banon. Cypress Grove's Humboldt Fog from Northern California is another delicious and beautiful choice; a mildly goaty cheese that intensifies with age, each wedge is accented by a line of edible, dark vegetable ash that recalls the area's morning fog.

Just about any style of blue cheese pairs well with sweet wines. Valdeon, a blue cheese from Spain, is rich and somewhat nutty with abundant blue veins. Cabrales is an intense Spanish blue that may be more widely available. A wonderfully rich and creamy blue for ending a meal is Saint Agur, a cow's milk cheese from Auvergne boasting 60 percent fat. We also love Cashel Blue from Ireland, and Point Reyes Farmstead Cheese Company's Original Blue from California, a rich, tangy blue made with raw milk from Holstein cows.

Almond Wafers

• • •

These spiced, almond-studded cookies are addictive. We love them on their own or as a crisp accompaniment to a creamy dessert. Keep some on hand in the freezer for fresh cookies at a moment's notice when guests knock at the door with a bottle of their favorite dessert wine.

MAKING THE MATCH

Almonds and spice are sherry's natural partners. We like these with cream sherry or a lush, ultra-sweet PX such as the single harvest Alvear Pedro Ximénez de Añada (Spain). A lingering almond finish pairs perfectly with the wafers.

1 cup sugar

2¾ cups all-purpose flour

¾ teaspoons baking soda

½ teaspoon ground cinnamon

¼ teaspoon freshly grated nutmeg

¼ teaspoon salt

¾ cup (1½ sticks) plus 2 table-spoons unsalted butter, at room temperature

¾ cup whole raw almonds

Line the bottom of an 8-inch square baking pan with a piece of plastic film long enough to extend up two sides of the pan. Stir the sugar and ⅓ cup water in a medium saucepan over low heat just long enough to dissolve the sugar. Cool to room temperature. Stir together the flour, baking soda, cinnamon, nutmeg, and salt; set aside.

Mix the butter at medium speed with an electric mixer until creamy. Mix in the cooled sugar-water until well blended, about 2 minutes. Add in the flour mixture at low speed to form a soft dough. Stir in the almonds just to incorporate them. (You may need to finish the mixing by hand.) Spread and press the dough evenly into the prepared pan, cover tightly with plastic film, and freeze until completely firm, about 3 hours.

Preheat the oven to 325 degrees F and position two racks in the upper and lower thirds of the oven. Line two baking sheets with parchment paper or silicone baking mats. Run a small paring knife around the edges of the pan to loosen the dough, then invert it onto a flat surface. Peel away the plastic film. With a sharp, heavy knife, cut the dough into four blocks that are 8 inches long and 2 inches wide. Wrap 3 of the blocks in plastic film and return them to the freezer. (The blocks can be wrapped tightly in plastic film and frozen for up to 3 months before slicing and baking.)

Cut the remaining block with a small paring knife into ¼-inch-thick slices. Arrange the wafers ½ inch apart on the baking sheets. Repeat with the remaining blocks of dough, removing each from the freezer as needed and putting the pans into the oven as they are filled. Bake the wafers until they are light golden, 15 to 20 minutes. Transfer the wafers to a rack to cool. Store the cooled cookies in an airtight container at room temperature for up to 2 weeks.

makes about 10 dozen small wafers

Caramel Macadamia Tart

• • •

We love the contrast of flavors and textures in this tart (see picture on page 7): toasty nuts, gooey-chewy caramel filling, and buttery pastry with a hint of crunch from cornmeal. The tart is just right at room temperature—served warm the filling will not be firm enough, while refrigerating it will harden the caramel.

MAKING THE MATCH

Because this tart is candy sweet, it needs a distinctly sweet wine. We like it with a Pedro Ximénez sherry, which marries beautifully with the rich caramel and nuts. It's also terrific with a 10-year tawny port or a 20-year Colheita, and one of our favorite matches is Blandy's 5-year-old Malmsey Madeira.

cornmeal crust

¾ cup (1½ sticks) unsalted butter, at room temperature

⅓ cup granulated sugar

1 large egg

1½ cups all-purpose flour

⅔ cup fine cornmeal

½ teaspoon salt

caramel macadamia filling

½ cup dark brown sugar, lightly packed

⅓ cup (⅔ stick) unsalted butter

¼ cup granulated sugar

3 tablespoons light corn syrup

¼ teaspoon salt

1 cup macadamia nuts, toasted and coarsely chopped (see page 139)

¼ cup cream

To make the crust: Beat together the butter and sugar until creamy, about 2 minutes, using a standing mixer with a paddle attachment. Add the egg and beat until smooth, scraping down the bowl with a rubber spatula. Add the flour, cornmeal, and salt at low speed until the mixture collects around the paddle. Turn out onto a floured surface and knead briefly. Cut the dough in half, flatten each half into a disk, wrap in plastic film, and refrigerate for at least 40 minutes or up to 3 days.

Preheat the oven to 350 degrees F. Have on hand a 9-inch fluted tart pan, about ¾ inch deep with a removable bottom.

To make the filling: Bring the brown sugar, butter, granulated sugar, corn syrup, and salt to a rolling boil, stirring over medium heat in a small, heavy saucepan. Boil 1 minute without stirring, then remove from the heat and stir in the nuts and cream. (The mixture may bubble up.) Set aside.

Roll one disk of dough into a 10-inch circle on a well-floured surface using a floured rolling pin. Use a flat, rimless baking sheet to transfer and center the pastry over the tart pan. Press the crust firmly into the bottom and sides of the pan, using dough scraps to repair any tears. It should extend a little beyond the rim of the pan to seal with the top crust. Pour the macadamia filling into the crust. Refrigerate the tart while you roll the top pastry.

Roll the second dough disk into a 10-inch circle. Center the top crust over the filling, then roll the pin firmly over the top of the pan to seal the crusts and neatly trim the edge. Pinch together any areas that are not well sealed. Cut a wide 1-inch slit in the center of the top crust.

Place the tart on a baking sheet and bake until the crust is golden, about 35 minutes. Transfer to a rack and cool for about 20 minutes. Remove the sides of the tart pan and let cool to room temperature. Transfer the tart to a serving platter and cut in small wedges with a sharp knife.

makes 12 servings

Classic Amaretti

. . .

In Italy, these little almond cookies are traditionally made using a combination of regular and bitter almonds, or sometimes apricot kernel paste. Mary first learned to make amaretti from Master Pastry Chef Albert Kumin at his International Pastry Arts Center in Bedford Hills, New York. Jennie learned a similar cookie as a child from her friend's father, Stanley Schear, who owned and operated Jespersen's Pastry Shop in Scarsdale, not far from Bedford Hills. These addictive amaretti start out with a crunch, then melt into a chewy-soft interior.

MAKING THE MATCH

Robust almond flavor makes these a natural match with a cream or sweet oloroso sherry. A Sauternes-style wine with citrus and apricot notes will deliciously intensify the almond in the cookies. Château Lamothe Guignard Sauternes (France) is a good choice.

10 tablespoons (7 ounces) almond paste

¼ cup granulated sugar

2 large egg whites

2 drops almond extract

Powdered sugar for finishing

Line two heavy baking sheets with parchment paper or silicone baking mats. Break the almond paste into small pieces in a mixing bowl. Add the sugar and mix at medium speed with a handheld electric mixer until well combined, about 1 minute. (Alternatively, this can be mixed in a food processor.) Add 1 egg white and continue to mix until the mixture begins to form a thick batter, about 1 minute, scraping down the sides of the bowl as needed. Beat in the second egg white and the almond extract. The mixture should be thick and smooth without any lumps of almond paste.

Spoon the batter into a pastry bag fitted with a ½-inch plain round tip. Pipe cookies in 1-inch mounds onto the prepared pan, leaving about an inch between them. (Alternatively, use a resealable plastic bag, cutting a tip off of one corner, or use wet hands to form 1-inch balls of the dough and press them onto the baking sheet with the palm of your hand to slightly flatten them.) Let the cookies stand uncovered at room temperature for at least 12 hours and no more than 24 hours to form a crunchy crust.

Preheat the oven to 375 degrees F and position two racks in the upper and lower thirds of the oven. Bake the cookies until they are golden brown, 15 to 20 minutes, rotating the sheets top to bottom and front to back after about 10 minutes. Transfer the sheets to cooling racks.

After about 2 minutes, carefully transfer the cookies with a spatula directly to the cooling rack. If any are difficult to remove from the parchment, allow the cookies to cool completely, then turn the parchment over onto a flat surface. Brush the back of the parchment with warm water, wait a minute, then try again.

Dust the amaretti with powdered sugar before serving. (The cookies can be stored in an airtight container for up to 1 week.)

makes about 3 dozen small amaretti

Toasted Pecan Sandies

• • •

Crunchy and buttery, these cookies will keep you reaching for more. Although you can use the same quantity of superfine or granulated sugar, powdered sugar produces the melt-in-your-mouth quality we love in these sandies. A European-style butter (see page 28) gives these cookies pure butter flavor.

MAKING THE MATCH

With their subdued sweetness, these cookies pair well with wines on the less-sweet end of the dessert wine spectrum. Their butter and salty pecan flavors and their crunchy, sandy texture match well with a wide range of wines. We love these with a Muscat de Beaumes-de-Venise such as the rich and elegant Domaine De Coyeux (France), or with a late harvest riesling or sémillon light on both oak and botrytis. They also pair well with a Madeira, vin santo, or sweet sherry.

2 cups all-purpose flour

½ teaspoon salt

1 cup (2 sticks) unsalted butter, at room temperature

½ cup powdered sugar

1¼ cup pecan pieces, toasted and coarsely chopped

Preheat the oven to 350 degrees F and position a rack near the center. Stir together the flour and salt; set aside. Using a standing mixer with a paddle attachment, beat the butter and sugar at medium speed until smooth and creamy, about 1 minute, scraping down the bowl occasionally. (Alternatively, these can be made using a handheld mixer or a wooden spoon.) Add the pecans and the flour mixture, mixing just until the ingredients come together. (The dough can be refrigerated, tightly wrapped, for up to 2 weeks, or rolled into a log approximately 1¼ inches in diameter and frozen; slice before baking.)

Roll a slightly heaping teaspoonful of dough into a ball and place it on an ungreased baking sheet. Flatten it with the palm of your hand. Continue making cookies, spacing them about an inch apart, until all the dough is used.

Bake the cookies until they are very light brown around the edges, 12 to 15 minutes. Transfer to a rack to cool. Store the cookies in an airtight container at room temperature for up to 2 weeks.

makes about 30 sandies

CHOCOLATE

Writer Calvin Trillin once reported that his four-year-old daughter, Abigail, after finishing a dish of chocolate ice cream, asserted, "My tongue is smiling." Indeed, chocolate may be the culinary manifestation of a grin. § While there appears to be widespread consensus regarding the virtues of chocolate, its pairing with wine is a subject of some debate among wine connoisseurs. Some dismiss the match, while others liken it to a taste of heaven. Fermentation and roasting turn the tannic and bitter cacao bean into the rich, mellow sweet we recognize as one of the world's most popular flavors. These qualities mimic similar flavors in dessert wines. § Chocolate and port are the classic pairing owing to their shared tannins and the chocolatey flavors that develop in sweet red wines. But don't stop there. Other fortified wines also make good matches, as do some of the port-style wines made from zinfandel, syrah, or other grapes. Banyuls and Maury, made in the southwest of France from the grenache grape, have deep berry and cocoa flavors. Another interesting match is dulce monastrell (*monastrell* is the Spanish name for the mourvèdre grape). These wines are all likely to provide a good alternative whenever a vintage port would pair well.

Research tells us that 14 out of any 10 individuals like chocolate.

— SANDRA BOYNTON, *CHOCOLATE: THE CONSUMING PASSION*

selecting chocolate

We are fortunate to have such a vast and growing selection of chocolate available. As with wine, taste in chocolate is very personal. Whether for nibbling or cooking, select a chocolate you love.

Our favorite brands for baking are Callebaut, Guittard (especially the E. Guittard line), and Valrhona (in particular, their Le Noir Gastronomie Dark Chocolate). Other good brands include Michel Cluizel, El Rey, Felchlin, and Scharffen Berger. Among brands widely available in supermarkets, choose bars of Hershey's Special Dark from the candy section over the boxed chocolate in the baking aisle. Chocolate chips contain ingredients that help them keep their shape when baked into cookies. Since these can compromise the texture of some desserts, avoid substituting chips for solid chocolate.

Cocoa is made by removing most of the cocoa butter from the cocoa mass, leaving behind a solid cake that is sifted into a fine powder. While Dutch-processed cocoa yields desserts with a dark color and mellow chocolate flavor, in most cases we prefer the more robust flavor of non-alkalized cocoa. Unless Dutch-processed is specified, use non-alkalized cocoa. Our favorite brands are Ghirardelli, Guittard, and Scharffen Berger.

Using Bittersweet Chocolate. When we call for bittersweet chocolate, we mean a high-quality chocolate labeled as having 55 to 62 percent cocoa mass, the combined mass of cocoa solids and cocoa butter. For our recipes, chocolate from 35 to 45 percent will contribute too much sugar and not enough chocolate flavor, while those having more than about 63 percent cocoa mass can dramatically alter the consistency of the finished dessert. If you have a higher percentage chocolate, use 3 ounces of your chocolate for every 4 ounces of bittersweet in our recipes, and add 1½ teaspoons of sugar for every ounce indicated in the original recipe.

Cocoa Walnut Biscotti

• • •

Tuscans claim the first biscotti were baked in the city of Prato in the 13th century. These are wonderful dipped in the traditional vin santo, though butter keeps this version tender and crumbly, even without a dunk.

MAKING THE MATCH

We like these with an orange muscat such as Quady Essensia (Madera, California) to bring out the hint of orange in the cookies. They are also delicious with ruby or tawny port, black muscat, cream sherry, or—of course—vin santo.

1¾ cups all-purpose flour

¼ cup unsweetened, Dutch-processed cocoa powder

1½ teaspoons baking powder

½ teaspoon baking soda

½ teaspoon salt

¾ cup sugar

6 tablespoons (¾ stick) unsalted butter, at room temperature

2 teaspoons finely grated orange zest

2 tablespoons fresh orange juice

2 large eggs

1½ cups walnut pieces, toasted and coarsely chopped (see page 139)

Preheat the oven to 325 degrees F and position two racks in the upper and lower thirds of the oven. Line a baking sheet with a silicone baking mat or parchment paper. Sift together the flour, cocoa, baking powder, baking soda, and salt. Set aside.

In a medium bowl, beat the sugar, butter, orange zest, and orange juice until smooth and creamy with a handheld electric mixer at medium speed. Add the eggs, one at a time, beating for 1 minute after each addition. Add the flour mixture and beat at low speed until the dough comes together into a soft mass. Mix in the walnuts.

Turn the sticky mass of dough out onto a floured surface and cut it into three pieces. Flour your hands and roll each piece into a log about 1½ inches wide. (Make the logs wider and flatter if you prefer longer finished biscotti.) The logs needn't be all the same length. Place them on the prepared pan, leaving about 2 inches between them to allow them to spread as they bake. (The unbaked logs can be frozen, tightly wrapped in aluminum foil, for up to two months.)

Bake the dough logs until the tops have formed a light crust and retain only a little impression when you press them lightly with your finger, about 25 minutes. Transfer the pan to a rack to cool. Reduce the oven to 275 degrees F.

When they are cool enough to handle, transfer the logs to a cutting board. Cut them with a serrated knife at a slight diagonal into ½-inch-thick slices. Lay the cookies flat on their sides on two baking sheets.

Bake the biscotti until the cut surfaces are dry to the touch and lightly toasted, about 25 minutes. Transfer to a rack to cool completely. The cookies will dry and crisp more as they cool. Store the cooled biscotti in an airtight container at room temperature for up to a month, or freeze them, tightly wrapped, and thaw at room temperature.

makes about 3 dozen biscotti

Blackberry Topped Chocolate Silk Tart

• • •

Blackberries provide a refreshing, sweet-tart contrast to the dense chocolate filling in this dessert. The fruit acts as a bridge between the tart and the wine, bringing out dark berry flavors in both. This dessert is as easy to prepare as it is elegant.

MAKING THE MATCH

Look for a sweet red wine with berry and chocolate flavors, such as a ruby or vintage port, or a port-style wine made from zinfandel or syrah grapes. We enjoy this with the berry and rose petal flavors in Rosenblum Cellars Black Muscat (Alameda, California).

pastry crust

½ cup (1 stick) unsalted butter, at room temperature, cut into 8 pieces

¼ cup sugar

1 large egg yolk

1¼ cups all-purpose flour

¼ teaspoon salt

chocolate silk filling

12 ounces bittersweet chocolate, finely chopped

1 cup heavy cream

2 tablespoons sugar

¼ teaspoon salt

½ cup (1 stick) unsalted butter, at room temperature, cut into 8 pieces

2 large egg yolks

½ cup sour cream

1 pint (2 cups) ripe blackberries for garnishing

To prepare the crust: Pulse the butter and sugar in a food processor until combined. Add the egg yolk and pulse a few times more. Add the flour and salt and process just until the dough balls up around the blades. Turn the dough out onto a floured surface and knead two or three times, then press it into a flat disk. Wrap in plastic film and refrigerate until firm, about 30 minutes.

Preheat the oven to 350 degrees F. Turn the dough onto a well-floured surface. With a floured rolling pin, carefully roll the dough into an 11½-inch circle, moving it frequently to be sure it does not stick. Use a flat, rimless baking sheet to transfer the pastry to an ungreased 10-inch tart pan with a removable bottom, centering the dough and pressing it firmly into the bottom and sides of the pan, and patching any tears with dough scraps. Roll the pin firmly over the top of the pan to neatly trim the edge. Bake until the crust is light golden brown, 20 to 25 minutes. Set the pan on a rack to cool completely.

While the pastry is baking, make the filling: Place the chocolate in a medium bowl. Bring the cream, sugar, and salt to a full, rolling boil in a saucepan. Pour the boiling cream over the chocolate and let it sit a few seconds to begin melting, then stir gently with a whisk just until the chocolate is smooth. Add the butter a tablespoon or two at a time and whisk until each piece is incorporated. Whisk in the egg yolks until smooth. Fold in the sour cream.

Pour the filling into the tart shell and set aside, uncovered, until it is completely cool and softly set, about 1 hour. (If not serving the tart within 2 hours, cover tightly and refrigerate for up to 1 week. Remove at least 30 minutes before serving to bring to room temperature.)

Remove the outer ring of the tart pan and transfer the tart to a serving platter. Decorate the top with blackberries, forming two concentric circles around the outer edge, plus a few berries in the center. Cut the tart with a sharp knife, dipping the blade in hot water and wiping it clean between slices.

makes 12 servings

Bittersweet Chocolate Hazelnut Torte with Brandied Currants and Orange

• • •

This rich, moist torte has a wonderful mix of textures and flavors—a tender chocolate crumb, toasted nuts, and plump currants infused with brandy and a hint of orange. It's worth splurging on the best quality chocolate. If the percentage of cocoa liquor is very high (65 to 72 percent), eliminate the ounce of unsweetened chocolate. This is a great make-ahead dessert, as it is even more delicious the second day. Because it contains no flour, it's a terrific choice for Passover (substitute additional orange juice or Passover wine for the brandy).

MAKING THE MATCH

The chocolate, toasted hazelnut, and brandy pair beautifully with a black muscat, such as Quady Vineyards' Elysium Black Muscat (Madera, California). The wine's floral nose and rose petal and chocolate flavors are a wonderful match. Highlight the nuts with a Madeira or cream sherry, the chocolate with a Banyuls, or both with a tawny port. If you serve the torte during Passover, consider Gan Eden Black Muscat (San Joaquin, California), which beautifully captures the typical perfume of the muscat grape.

⅓ cup dried currants

2 tablespoons brandy

1 tablespoon finely grated orange zest

2 tablespoons fresh orange juice

Butter and flour for pan

¾ cup hazelnuts, toasted and skinned (see page 139)

2 tablespoons plus ½ cup granulated sugar

5 ounces bittersweet chocolate, coarsely chopped

1 ounce unsweetened chocolate, coarsely chopped

2 tablespoons unsalted butter

4 large eggs, at room temperature

¼ teaspoon salt

Powdered sugar or whipped cream for finishing

Stir together the currants, brandy, orange zest, and orange juice in a small bowl. Press the currants into the liquid to make sure they are submerged, and set aside.

Preheat the oven to 325 degrees F and position a rack near the center. Generously butter the sides only of a 9-by-2-inch round cake pan, preferably nonstick. Dust the buttered sides with flour, tapping out any excess. Line the bottom with a circle of parchment paper and butter the top of the parchment.

Grind the hazelnuts in a food processor with 2 tablespoons of the sugar as finely as possible, taking care not to make nut butter. (Nut pieces larger than coarse sand will make the cake crumbly and difficult to cut.) Set aside.

Melt the bittersweet and unsweetened chocolates with the 2 tablespoons butter in a small, heavy saucepan over low heat. Using a standing mixer with a whisk attachment or a handheld electric mixer, whip the eggs, salt, and remaining ½ cup of sugar in a large bowl at high speed until very thick and pale and about triple in volume, 8 to 10 minutes, scraping down the bowl with a spatula as needed. At low speed, mix in the reserved currants with their soaking liquid, the ground nuts, and the melted chocolate until well incorporated.

Pour the batter into the prepared pan and bake until the top feels firm when lightly pressed with your finger near the center, about 30 minutes. The center should not appear sunken when you remove it from the oven, though it will sink a little as it cools. Place the pan on a rack until completely cool, about 1 hour.

This delicate cake takes a bit of care to prevent crumbling; be sure it is completely cool before unmolding and serving. Loosen the torte from the sides of the pan by running a knife around the edges. Place a plate over the pan and hold them tightly together as you invert the torte onto the plate. If it sticks, firmly tap the bottom of the pan until you hear the cake drop to the plate. Carefully remove the pan and pull the parchment paper from the cake. Invert the cake a second time onto a serving platter so that it is right-side up.

Generously dust the cake with powdered sugar or spread with whipped cream just before serving. Run a sharp knife under hot water and use the wet knife to cut straight down into the torte in a single stroke, then slide the knife out toward you (not back up). Wipe the knife with a cloth and dip in hot water between slices.

makes 10 servings

Chocolate Soufflé Roulade

• • •

This moist chocolate cake wrapped around a fluffy cocoa cream filling is considerably easier to prepare than it appears. The tender cake rolls beautifully, while the cocoa stabilizes the filling, allowing the cake to be assembled ahead and refrigerated. We recommend a chocolate with 50 to 60 percent cocoa mass; higher percentage chocolates weigh down this airy cake.

MAKING THE MATCH

We love this with all the chocolate-friendly wines: vintage port, zinfandel port, Banyuls, and the mourvèdre-based dulce monastrell. The ruby-hued Bodegas Olivares Dulce Monastrell (Jumilla, Spain) is like a vintage port but with lower alcohol, so it won't overwhelm the cake's light texture. The wine's dried fruit, balsamic, and spice notes give the roulade an extra flavor boost.

roulade

2 ounces bittersweet chocolate, melted and cooled to room temperature (see page 34)

2 large egg yolks

¼ teaspoon salt

¾ cup granulated sugar

7 large egg whites

¼ cup cake flour, sifted

cream filling

2 cups heavy cream

⅓ cup unsweetened cocoa powder

3 tablespoons granulated or superfine sugar

Powdered sugar for finishing

Strawberries, raspberries, or chocolate curls (see page 169) for finishing

Preheat the oven to 425 degrees F and position a rack in the lower third of the oven. Line a 17-by-12-inch rimmed baking sheet or jelly-roll pan with parchment paper.

To prepare the cake: Whisk together the chocolate, egg yolks, salt, and 2 tablespoons warm water in a large bowl. Set aside. Stir the granulated sugar and ¼ cup water in a small saucepan over medium heat to dissolve the sugar. Remove from heat and let cool slightly.

Whip the egg whites at high speed until they are very foamy and just beginning to form soft peaks. Slowly drizzle in the warm sugar syrup as you continue to whip until the whites form medium peaks that hold their shape but are not at all stiff or dry.

Use a spatula or handheld whisk to gently stir one-third of the egg whites into the chocolate mixture. Gently fold in the flour and then the remaining egg whites. Immediately spread the batter evenly into the prepared pan. Bake until

the cake springs back when you press it lightly in the center, about 15 minutes. Do not be concerned if the cake puffs in places; it will settle as it cools. Transfer the pan to a rack and let the cake cool completely.

To prepare the filling: In a medium bowl, combine the cream, cocoa powder, and granulated or superfine sugar. Whip the filling to firm peaks, starting at slow speed and increasing to medium-high as it thickens.

Run a sharp knife around the edge of the cooled cake, then invert the cake onto a piece of parchment paper on a flat surface. Carefully peel the parchment paper from the bottom of the cake. Spread the filling evenly over the cake, making sure to go all the way to the edges.

With a short side of the cake facing you, tuck ½ inch of the cake's edge tightly over the filling, then begin to roll, using the parchment to help form a tight roll. Pull away the parchment as you roll to prevent rolling it into the

cake. Trim the ends of the roll, cutting at a slight angle. (The cake can be tightly wrapped and refrigerated for up to 4 days or frozen for up to 2 weeks; leave wrapped while thawing in the refrigerator.)

Transfer the cake to a serving platter. Just before serving, sift powdered sugar over the top. Cut the cake into slices about 1 inch thick on a slight angle using a thin, sharp or serrated knife. Garnish with berries or chocolate curls.

makes 8 servings

White Chocolate Raspberry Parfait

• • •

In the United States, we generally think of a parfait as a layered dessert made with ice cream, fruits or syrups, and whipped cream. The French have something else in mind. Though also served in a tall, narrow sundae glass, the classic *parfait* (French for "perfect") is a frozen custard made using the technique for sabayon. The resulting treat freezes creamy smooth without needing an ice-cream maker. Use white chocolate made with cocoa butter for the best flavor.

MAKING THE MATCH

This blond dessert with chocolate flavor notes matches well with a young, fruity, lower-alcohol zinfandel port. The wine brings out the chocolatey flavors in the dessert and pairs well with the raspberries. It is also nice with Muscat de Beaumes-de-Venise or other muscats. We enjoy it with Montevina Aleatico (Amador County, California), a light-bodied muscat with a brilliant ruby hue.

2 large eggs

2 large egg yolks

¼ cup sugar

3 ounces white chocolate, melted (see page 34)

1 cup heavy cream, whipped to medium peaks

1 pint (2 cups) fresh raspberries

Raspberry liqueur for drizzling (optional)

Combine the eggs, egg yolks, and sugar in the top of a double boiler and place over, but not touching, about an inch of simmering water. While whisking briskly and constantly, heat the mixture until it is hot and has turned from liquid to all foam, about 5 minutes. Remove from the heat and stir in the melted chocolate.

Beat the egg and chocolate mixture with an electric mixer at high speed until it is room temperature, 3 to 5 minutes. Fold in the whipped cream. Transfer to a covered 1-quart container and freeze until firm enough to scoop, 2 to 3 hours or up to 1 month.

Alternate layers of the white chocolate parfait and berries in tall sundae glasses. Drizzle the tops with raspberry liqueur, if desired.

makes 6 servings

Triple Chocolate Buttermilk Loaf Cake

• • •

A touch of vanilla enhances the rich flavor from three types of chocolate in this cake: cocoa, bittersweet, and chips. Tangy buttermilk complements the chocolate and keeps the cake moist. For the best texture, bring all the ingredients to room temperature before mixing. To gild the lily, finish the cake with a simple chocolate glaze (see page 168).

MAKING THE MATCH

A moist and densely chocolate cake, we love it with all the usual chocolate matches: Banyuls, zinfandel port, vintage (or LBV) port, or ruby port. Rosenblum Cellars Zinfandel Port, Carapinha Vineyard (California), makes a lovely match.

Butter and flour for pan

1½ cups all-purpose flour

⅓ cup unsweetened cocoa powder

¾ teaspoon baking powder

½ teaspoon baking soda

½ teaspoon salt

½ cup (1 stick) unsalted butter, at room temperature

1 cup sugar

½ teaspoon pure vanilla extract

3 large eggs

2 ounces bittersweet chocolate, melted and cooled to room temperature (see page 34)

1 cup buttermilk

½ cup bittersweet or semisweet chocolate chips

Preheat the oven to 350 degrees F and position a rack near the center. Butter and flour a 9-by-5-by-3-inch metal loaf pan.

Sift together the flour, cocoa, baking powder, baking soda, and salt; set aside. Beat together the butter, sugar, and vanilla at medium speed using a standing mixer with the paddle attachment until very creamy, about 4 minutes. Add the eggs, one at a time, incorporating each completely before adding the next and scraping down the bowl between additions. Stir in the melted chocolate. (Alternatively, use a handheld electric mixer.)

Stir in half of the flour mixture, then the buttermilk, then the remaining flour, mixing each time just until all the ingredients are incorporated. Stir in the chocolate chips.

Spread the batter into the prepared pan and smooth the top. Bake until the cake springs back when pressed lightly near the center and a toothpick inserted about 1 inch from the edge emerges clean, 55 to 60 minutes. Transfer the pan to a rack and cool to room temperature.

Run a sharp knife around the sides of the pan and invert, tapping the bottom of the pan if needed to release the cake. Place the cake right-side up on a serving plate and cut it into 1-inch slices with a sharp knife. (Store the cake at room temperature, tightly wrapped, for up to 4 days, or freeze for up to a month.)

makes 8 servings

CARAMEL SAUCE 168 :: CHOCOLATE GLAZE 168 :: FRUIT PURÉES 168 :: CHOCOLATE CURLS 169
CAKE STENCILS 169 :: OTHER FINISHING TOUCHES 169

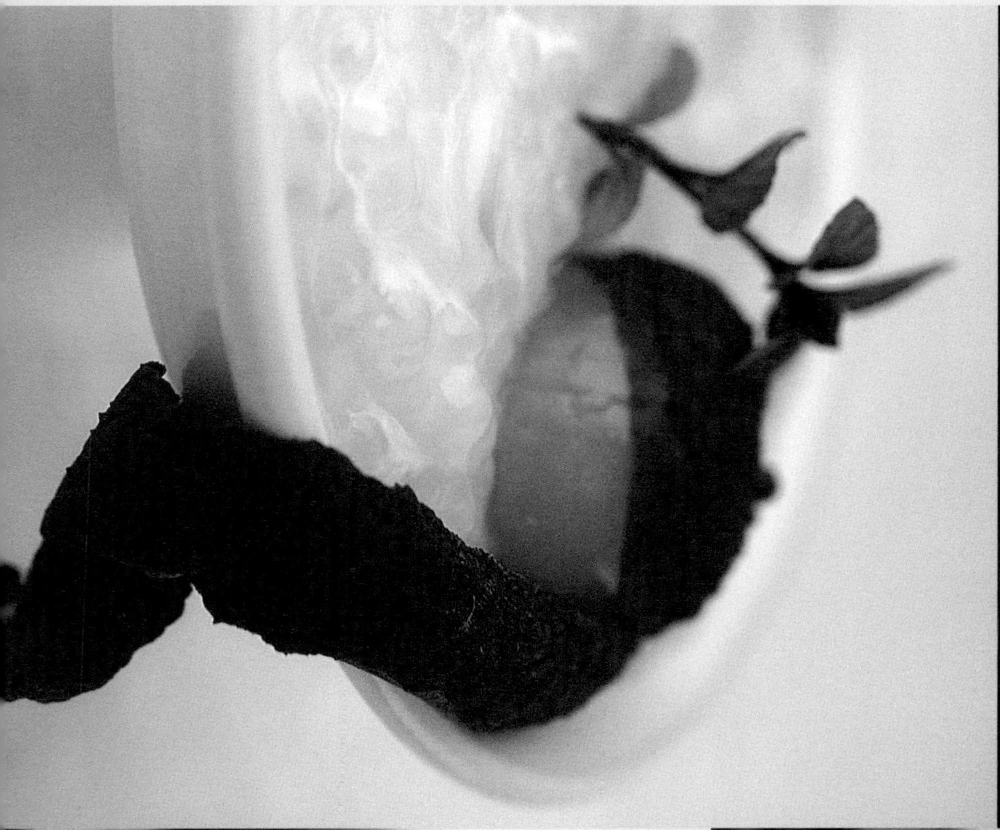

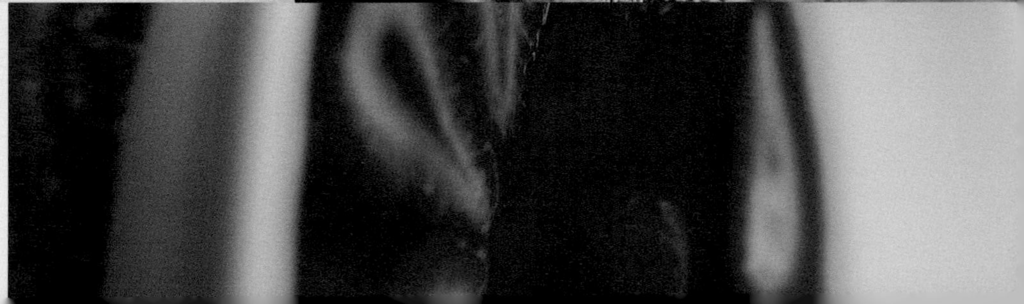

FINISHING TOUCHES

A small embellishment can make even the simplest dessert seem decadent. Many also enhance the pairing with wines. § Use sauces to garnish finished desserts or to decorate the plates on which you serve them. Make sure sauces are perfectly smooth, as lumps can clog a pastry tip or bottle opening. § For a simple decoration, spoon the sauce into a pastry bag fitted with the smallest round tip and pipe squiggles or zigzag lines across the dessert, or on the plate before topping with a serving of the dessert. Alternatively, spoon the sauce into a resealable plastic sandwich bag, carefully pressing out the air before zipping it closed. Taking care not to spill out the contents, snip a small opening in a bottom corner. Hold the bag over the dessert or plate and squeeze out the contents with even pressure. § Squeeze bottles can be used in much the same way. Fill the bottle, cut the tip to the desired size, invert the bottle, and squeeze over the dessert or plate. § To create a pool of sauce beneath a dessert, spoon about ¼ cup of the sauce onto a dessert plate, then swirl the plate or use the back of the spoon to spread it over a larger area. Center the dessert on top of the sauce. § Following are some of our favorite sauces and decorating techniques.

The friendly cow, all red and white,

I love with all my heart;

She gives me cream with all her might,

To eat with apple tart.

— ROBERT LOUIS STEVENSON, "THE COW"

caramel sauce

Heat 1 cup of heavy cream to a simmer in a small saucepan; set aside. Melt 3 tablespoons unsalted butter with ¼ teaspoon salt in a medium, heavy anodized aluminum or stainless-steel saucepan. Stir in ¾ cup sugar and cook over medium-high heat, whisking constantly, until the sugar dissolves and the mixture turns a deep amber, about 5 minutes. Remove from the heat and pour in the warm cream, taking care to keep your distance—it will steam furiously. Wait 30 seconds for the steam to subside, then whisk the caramel until it is completely smooth. If bits of caramel harden, stir the sauce over low heat to melt them.

chocolate glaze

Bring ½ cup heavy cream and 1 tablespoon light corn syrup to a simmer over low heat, stirring to dissolve the syrup. Remove from the heat and add 4 ounces of chopped bittersweet chocolate. Wait 1 minute for the chocolate to begin melting, then whisk gently to smooth the glaze. Cool a few minutes until it is slightly thickened but still pourable. Pour and spread the glaze over a cooled cake set on a rack over a plate to catch the dripping chocolate. Leave the glaze to set at least 1 hour before serving.

fruit purées

Use ripe, juicy fruits such as berries, mangoes, peaches, or plums. If the fruit has a peel, remove it. Pulse 1 to 2 cups of fruit in a food processor with sugar and lemon or lime juice to taste until it is nearly smooth, adding a little water or fruit juice if needed. Press the purée through a fine-mesh strainer with the back of a spoon and stir in additional sugar or lemon juice if needed.

chocolate curls

Warm a block of chocolate at least 1 inch thick in the microwave on high power for 20 seconds. Continue heating in 10 second increments until the chocolate is slightly softened but not melting. Hold the softened chocolate in one hand and use the other to pull a sharp vegetable peeler along the side of the block of chocolate. If the chocolate becomes too firm, re-warm it for a few seconds in the microwave.

Carefully pick up the soft curls with a toothpick or spatula to avoid breaking them. Refrigerate to keep them firm until needed, or freeze them in an airtight container for up to 1 month.

cake stencils

For a simple cake-top decoration, place a doily or other paper cutout or stencil on top of the cake and sift powdered sugar or cocoa (or a mixture of the two) evenly over the cake's surface. Lift off the stencil to reveal the design, taking care not to spill excess sugar or cocoa back onto the cake.

other finishing touches

A light dusting of powdered sugar or cocoa, a scoop of ice cream, or a dollop of crème fraîche, lightly sweetened whipped cream, or sweetened sour cream add easy elegance. Try decorating desserts with fresh edible flowers, grown without pesticides or potentially harmful chemicals, or embellish platters or individual servings with chopped, toasted nuts or diced fruits that complement the dessert.

Beerenauslese

[BAY-ruhn-OWS-lay-zuh]

German for "selected berries," this is the second to top level of sugar at harvest among the country's six designated levels.

Botrytis cinerea

[boh-TRI-tihs sihn-EHR-ee-uh]

Known as the noble rot, this mold develops on grapes and creates, under the right conditions, intensely sweet and aromatic wines.

Brix

[BRIHKS]

Named for a nineteenth-century German inventor, the Brix scale measures the amount of sugar in grapes and wine. One degree Brix equals 1 gram of sugar per 100 grams of grape juice.

Muscat

[MUHS-kat; MUHS-kuht]

A family of grapes that includes hundreds of varietals, many used in making sweet wines with a characteristic perfumed quality. Common varietals include the brown muscat of Australia and muscat blanc à petits grains ("white muscat with little berries"), also known as moscato bianco and muscat canelli. Orange muscat often tastes as if orange essence were added. Black muscat produces a sweet wine with a taste of blackberries and a fragrance of rose petals.

Riesling

[REEZ-ling; REES-ling]

Regarded as one of the world's most important wine grapes, riesling is used to produce many sweet wines, especially in Germany, Austria, and Alsace. The grape also goes by White Riesling or Johannisberg Riesling. Gray Riesling is a different varietal altogether.

Sauternes

[soh-TEHRN]

Located in France's Bordeaux region, Sauternes is one of the world's most famous sweet wine appellations; Chateau d'Yquem is its most esteemed producer. The wines are made predominantly from botrytised sémillon and sauvignon blanc grapes. Avoid confusing it with the indifferent and unrelated sauterne, which has no "s" at the end.

Sherry

This fortified wine originated in the area around Jerez in Spain's southern Andalusia region. The wines range from dry to intensely sweet. Oxidation gives them their typical deep golden color and rich, nutty aromas and flavors. The sweetest sherries are full-flavored oloroso, cream sherry, and the ultra-sweet Pedro Ximénez, or PX, often blended with dry sherry to sweeten it.

Trockenbeerenauslese

[TRAWK-uhn-bay-ruhn-OWS-lay-zuh]

Translated as "dry selected berries," these German wines are made from ultra-ripe, botrytised grapes. Balancing acidity prevents the viscous wines from tasting cloying. Expensive to produce, they can rank among the world's greatest sweet wines.

SOURCES

Bridge Kitchenware
212-688-4220
www.bridgekitchenware.com
Extensive collection of cooking, baking, and pastry equipment, from accessories to appliances.

Broadway Panhandler
866-266-5927
www.broadwaypanhandler.com
Broad selection of bakeware, cookware, kitchen tools, and tabletop supplies.

Chocosphere
877-992-4626
www.chocosphere.com
Wide variety of chocolates from around the world, including some organic selections.

K&L Wine Merchants
800-247-5987
www.klwines.com
Wine, glassware, and wine information.

Kerekes Bakery & Restaurant Equipment, Inc.
800-525-5556
www.bakedeco.com
Baking and pastry tools and supplies, some geared toward professionals but with plenty to offer for the home kitchen.

King Arthur Flour
800-827-6836
www.kingarthurflour.com
Information about baking, as well as flour and other baking ingredients and equipment.

NY Cake and Baking Distributor
800-942-2539
www.nycake.com
Chocolate in bulk, as well as almond paste and other ingredients and a huge assortment of baking equipment and supplies.

Penzeys Spices
800-741-7787
www.penzeys.com
Quality herbs, spices, extracts, and seasonings.

Sur La Table
800-243-0852
www.surlatable.com
Assortment of bakeware, cookware, and kitchen accessories available in retail stores, by mail-order catalog, and online.

The Spanish Table
206-682-2827
www.spanishtable.com
Spanish and Portuguese wines, including port, sherry, and Madeira, available online and at stores in Seattle, Berkeley, and Santa Fe.

The Vanilla.COMpany
800-757-7511
www.vanilla.com
Vanilla facts, lore, and tips, as well as vanilla products.

Williams-Sonoma
877-812-6235
www.williams-sonoma.com
Bakeware, wine glasses, and other kitchen and tableware available in retail stores, by mail-order catalog, and online.

Wine Appreciation Guild
800-231-9463
www.wineappreciation.com
Publishes and distributes books on wine, and sells wine education materials, accessories, and storage devices.

Zachys Wine Online
800-723-0241
www.zachys.com
This wine shop offers one of the largest selections of wines online, as well as glassware, wine auctions, and live help during selected hours.

Many wineries have Web sites with information about their wines and how to obtain them; your favorite search engine is a good place to start.

BIBLIOGRAPHY

We found the following books helpful as we wrote this one.

Blom, Philip. *The Wines of Austria*. New York: Faber and Faber, 2000.

Corriher, Shirley O. *Cookwise: The Hows and Whys of Successful Cooking*. New York: William Morrow & Co., 1997.

Fletcher, Janet. *Fresh from the Farmers' Market: Year-round Recipes for the Pick of the Crop*. San Francisco: Chronicle Books, 1997.

Goodbody, Mary, Carolyn Miller, and Thy Tran. *Williams-Sonoma Kitchen Companion: The A to Z Guide to Everyday Cooking, Equipment & Ingredients*. San Francisco: Weldon Owen Inc. and Williams-Sonoma Inc., 2000.

Herbst, Ron and Sharon Tyler Herbst. *The New Wine Lover's Companion*. 2nd ed. Hauppauge, NY: Barron's Educational Series, 2003.

Herbst, Sharon Tyler. *The New Food Lover's Companion*. 3rd ed. Hauppauge, NY: Barron's Educational Series, 2001.

———. *The New Food Lover's Tiptionary*. New York: HarperCollins, 2002.

Jeffs, Julian. *Sherry*. Boston: Faber and Faber, 1992.

———. *The Wines of Spain*. New York: Faber and Faber, 1999.

Lambert-Gocs, Miles. *The Wines of Greece*. Boston: Faber and Faber, 1990.

Malgieri, Nick. *Chocolate: From Simple Cookies to Extravagant Showstoppers*. New York: HarperCollins, 1998.

McGee, Harold. *On Food and Cooking: The Science and Lore of the Kitchen*. New York: Fireside, 1997.

Parsons, Russ. *How to Read a French Fry: And Other Stories of Intriguing Kitchen Science*. New York: Houghton Mifflin, 2001.

Peterson, James. *Sweet Wines: A Guide to the World's Best with Recipes*. New York: Stewart, Tabori & Chang, 2002.

Robinson, Jancis, ed. *The Oxford Companion to Wine*. 2nd ed. Oxford, England: Oxford University Press, 1999.

Werlin, Laura. *The All American Cheese and Wine Book: Pairings, Profiles & Recipes*. New York: Stewart, Tabori & Chang, 2003.

We also found guidance in selected issues of *Cook's Illustrated* magazine.

THE WINE LOVER'S DESSERT COOKBOOK

TABLE OF EQUIVALENTS

The exact equivalents in the following tables have been rounded for convenience.

Liquid/Dry Measures

U.S.	Metric
¼ teaspoon	1.25 milliliters
½ teaspoon	2.5 milliliters
1 teaspoon	5 milliliters
1 tablespoon (*3 teaspoons*)	15 milliliters
1 fluid ounce (*2 tablespoons*)	30 milliliters
¼ cup	60 milliliters
⅓ cup	80 milliliters
½ cup	120 milliliters
1 cup	240 milliliters
1 pint (*2 cups*)	480 milliliters
1 quart (*4 cups, 32 ounces*)	960 milliliters
1 gallon (*4 quarts*)	3.84 liters

U.S.	Metric
1 ounce (*by weight*)	28 grams
1 pound	454 grams
2.2 pounds	1 kilogram

Oven Temperature

Fahrenheit	Celsius	Gas
250	120	½
275	140	1
300	150	2
325	160	3
350	180	4
375	190	5
400	200	6
425	220	7
450	230	8
475	240	9
500	260	10

Length

U.S.	Metric
⅛ inch	3 millimeters
¼ inch	6 millimeters
½ inch	12 millimeters
1 inch	2.5 centimeters